Dodie Zaugg ?

Draw
Near
Unto
Me

Draw Near Unto Me

JILL TODD BANFIELD

*GETTING CLOSER
TO GOD THROUGH
PRAYER AND
PERSONAL REVELATION*

Bookcraft
Salt Lake City, Utah

Library of Congress Catalog Card Number: 83-70816
ISBN O-88494-484-0

First Printing, 1983

Lithographed in the United States of America
PUBLISHERS PRESS
Salt Lake City, Utah

To those who are
struggling and yet reaching
for a better understanding of the skills of
prayer and personal revelation

Contents

Preface

The initial inspiration for this book came while serving my mission. My companion and I were asked to give a presentation on prayer to a group of missionaries in our district. As we prepared for the meeting we discussed some of the questions and struggles we were experiencing in our personal prayers. The essence of our frustrations centered in our inability to communicate with Heavenly Father. We felt that our words were not reaching his ears and that his revelations were not clear to our understandings.

In an effort to resolve our problem we decided to study the lives and prayers of those who had successfully communed with God to see if we could gain insight from their experiences. As we began to piece together the information we obtained, a pattern emerged. We discovered that those who successfully communicated with God were basically following a similar sequence of steps. We listed those steps and began to ponder them and experiment with them. As we did this, our ability to communicate increased. We were thrilled and comforted as we caught this new vista of understanding. The effects of applying this new knowledge to our personal prayers were fulfilling. For me, the most exciting results were breaking through the barriers that had thwarted my previous prayers and finding new confidence in my ability to hear and understand God's revelations to me.

Later as we discussed our "new knowledge" with the Elders in our district, we found they were having similar problems with their personal prayers. We bore testimony of how the application of these principles had enriched our individual prayers and challenged them to try using them. The response was overwhelming. All remarked on the greater success they had found in personal prayer.

On many occasions since my mission I have shared similar discussions. A common thread of frustration and concern has been expressed by people as they have tried to make prayer a living principle in their own lives. Many have said that as they have learned and applied these principles they have enjoyed greater fulfillment in their personal prayers.

The desire to write this book has grown out of my experiences and the experiences others have shared. This is one way for me to reach out to others who are struggling to have meaningful prayer.

Acknowledgments

A special thanks and acknowledgment is due the following people:

Julie McKenzie, who was my mission companion when the inspiration found in this book was received.

Rob Banfield, my husband, for his love and his encouragement to me to have a special project (this book) that would provide an extra dimension of joy in each day.

Ralph and Afton Todd and Phillip and Harriette Banfield for their love and for their excitement and support in this writing project.

Beth Bartel for the spiritual awareness she has developed and the time she donated to editing and typing the manuscript.

Dorothy Tomilson for her intellectual abilities and the time she devoted to reviewing and typing the manuscript and making suggestions.

Draw Near Unto Me...

Opening my bedroom door, I fell on the bed. My eyes welled up with tears as I again reviewed the events of the day and wondered: Why had God let me down? My goal for the past three and one-half years of high school had been to earn an all A, B report card. I began every semester with the determination to attain this goal, but to my disappointment there was always one C that crept in and I had to abandon my goal until the next semester. This had been my last semester, my last chance to attain my unfulfilled goal. I had resolved that this time I was going to do it! The term had progressed better than planned, and as the final week arrived I realized that I had really outdone myself. I was certain of As in all my classes but one, shorthand.

With my goal so near I went to my shorthand teacher to discuss my grade. She pointed out that pending the final, I could receive an A, B, or C. The thought of finally conquering this challenge excited me so much that I spent the next few days in a constant round of taking dictation and translating. The day of the final arrived. In my prayer that morning I specifically made it clear that I needed special help on my shorthand test. Then just to make sure the Lord realized I was serious about this, I decided to fast.

In spite of my prayers and preparation the final was a disaster. My goal was shattered, never to be fulfilled. I had no words to say to the Lord that afternoon as I broke my fast. I felt that my faith had been betrayed. I couldn't help thinking that if he didn't care enough to answer my prayer to complete what I thought was a worthy goal, then I didn't need to waste my time asking.

Perhaps you can reflect on similar struggles when you believed you had sincerely knocked at the Lord's door and, because it seemed to remain closed, you questioned why. For me, this was the first time I had been left with wondering questions: Why should I pray if it seems my prayers are in vain? Why should I pray if God is going to do as he chooses? Why should I bother to pray when I can't understand the answers and wonder if I ever will?

Before considering questions like these, I feel it important to say that my experience did not end here. The Lord was very aware of my emotions and my feelings of rejection and discouragement. Perhaps his desire to awaken me to the fact that he still loved and cared about me prompted the events which occurred later that day.

To celebrate the last day of school, my friends and I went swimming that afternoon. As I came up from the first dive I realized I hadn't removed my contact lenses before entering the pool, and they were no longer in my eyes. Instead of being devastated as I normally would have been, a comforting feeling began to fill my being and a voice came to my mind telling me not to worry, everything would be all right. Surprisingly I hardly took notice of the loss and continued having a great time.

Then unexpectedly the chlorine man came (he was a day early) to treat the pool, and our visit was cut short. He overheard me half jokingly tell the pool owner that if some contacts turned up in his filter they were mine. In a few minutes he returned and asked, "Did someone say she had lost some contacts?" I answered yes, and he replied, "I think I found them." We rushed back to the pool, and there in the bottom of the deep end about six inches apart were two brown specks—my contact lenses. I couldn't believe it. I was thrilled!

Upon returning home I related the story to my mother. It was then that the whole day's events came into perspective, and

I understood that the Lord was telling me that he still loved and cared about me and that there was a purpose in the disappointment I had experienced in falling short of my goal, a purpose which I did not yet understand.

It is comforting to realize that no matter how frustrated we feel when facing trials, the Lord loves us and has a purpose in how he chooses to respond to our prayers. In view of our finite perspective it is important that we are not quick to murmur or to become disillusioned when the Lord's intent is not clear to us while in the midst of our trials. As I learned from the grade incident, sometimes years pass before hindsight reveals his purpose.

Three years later as I entered college I had a renewed determination toward my goal. In fact, I desired to reach beyond the high-school goal. Now I wanted an all-A report card. From the first day of class I put a total effort into achieving my ambition. At the end of my freshman year I was thrilled to finally see the fulfillment of my goal. My grade point average was 4.0. As I look back on the total experience I believe that perhaps I would not have been as determined to succeed if I had reached my goal before college. The achieving of this goal at this period in my life was especially beneficial because it helped me obtain scholarships which aided in meeting college costs.

Knowing there is purpose in our trials, however, does not dispel the frustrations and questions that arise when trying to understand why our prayers seem futile and personal revelations appear nonexistent. Prayer experiences of my own and of others have convinced me that there is a need to look more deeply at the questions we have concerning the principles of prayer — the way they work and the struggles we face as we try to master them.

First, it is essential to realize that we cannot ignore or give up on prayer. Prayer plays a vital role in helping us find happiness in this life and achieve exaltation in the next life. President Marion G. Romney explains: "We should pray because prayer is indispensable to the accomplishment of the real purpose of our lives. We are children of God. As such, we have the potentiality to rise to his perfection. . . . No one shall ever reach such perfection unless he is guided to it by Him who is perfect. And that guidance from Him is to be had only through prayer." ("Prayer Is the Key," *Ensign*, Jan. 1976, p. 2.)

Second, the struggles we have while mastering the skill of two-way communication are part of a molding process in which the Lord shapes and perfects our character to prepare us for godhood.

Since prayer plays such an important part in our attainment of perfection, it is imperative that we learn to use it effectively. Many of us have the false assumption that competency in offering prayers and in understanding answers comes naturally. This is not so. Effective prayer is a process not an event. It entails developing an ability or skill. As in our developing any skill, success comes through continual practice.

Communication implies that we must talk to God and he with us. True communication involves each party in speaking and listening. Therefore a portion of time during prayer must be devoted to pondering and listening as well as to speaking. This allows God the opportunity to talk to us. When God communicates with us, it can be termed personal revelation.

Actually experiencing the two-way communication of prayer and personal revelation may initially appear to be an unreachable goal. Nevertheless I believe we can have this type of communication with God: first, by becoming aware of the elements or laws that govern prayer and personal revelation, and second, by putting them into consistent daily practice. Elder Bruce R. McConkie said that we must "learn and live the law of prayer so that we . . . can go where he [Jesus Christ] and his Father are." ("Why the Lord Ordained Prayer," *Ensign*, Jan. 1976, p. 8.)

Perhaps you have wondered: How do I break through barriers, such as time, circumstances, and the "ceiling," and rise above the habitual or dutiful prayer to a level wherein I truly communicate with God? How do I come to feel confident about my ability to hear and to understand God's revelations and to know how to apply his will in my life?

The purpose of this book is to present in a logical and workable manner the principles involved in prayer. It also analyzes some concepts and examples that can help us recognize and understand personal revelation. It breaks down communicating with God into ten steps. The chapters appear in the order in which they are best used to assure communication.

The principle of prayer is one of the most precious gifts the Lord has given us. Our understanding that we can communicate with our creator can change our lives.

Preparing for Prayer \quad *Chapter 1*

When I was young the one thing the kids in my neighborhood loved to do was build forts. We would build forts by piling tumbleweeds on top of each other, fitting cardboard boxes together, or digging holes and tunnels in the dirt. Once we tried to nail together some old scrap lumber, but somehow none of these methods seemed to create our dream fort. My dad must have felt sorry for us, because one Saturday he announced that he would help us build a fort. He started building in a very peculiar manner. Instead of just nailing some wood together for sides and a roof, he built a framelike structure with some crosspieces. He explained that this was the foundation. (We had never thought of that.) Then he did the same thing with the sides and roof. We were amazed, when we finally got to walk inside, that it didn't wobble and creak. The neighborhood kids all agreed that it was the best fort we'd ever had.

THE FOUNDATION MATERIALS

The key difference between our dream fort and all the others we had made was in the strong foundation. Likewise in prayer the key difference between a complacent or ritualistic prayer and a successful two-way communication with God is found in the foundation we build. Done prior to prayer, this foundation is the spiritual preparation that will invite and provide for the growth of the Lord's Spirit.

PRIVACY

The question naturally arises: What kind of things are needed to build a foundation that will prepare us to speak with God? Building "materials" such as place, privacy, opportunity to speak aloud, and atmosphere should be considered. Joseph Smith included them in his account of the First Vision:

> After I had retired to the place where I *had previously designed to go,* having looked around me, and *finding myself alone,* I kneeled down and began to offer up the *desires* of my heart to God. . . . It was the first time in my life that I had made such an attempt, for amidst all my anxieties I had never as yet made the attempt to *pray vocally.* (Joseph Smith—History 1:15, 14; italics added.)

President Spencer W. Kimball emphasizes:

> Prayer in solitude is rich and profitable. Praying alone helps us to shed shame or pretense, any lingering deceit; it helps us open our hearts and be totally honest and honorable in expressing all of our hopes and attitudes.
>
> I have long been impressed about the need for privacy in our personal prayers. The Savior at times found it necessary to slip away into the mountains or desert to pray. Similarly, the Apostle Paul turned to the desert and solitude after his great call. Enos found himself in solitary places to commune with God. . . .
>
> We, too, ought to find, where possible, a room, a corner, a closet, a place where we can "retire" to "pray vocally" in secret. ("Pray Always," *Ensign*, Oct. 1981, p. 4.)

PONDERING

Pondering or meditating is another aid in building a foundation for prayer. It can help to clear out the rubble of the day. (I've found that pondering is aided by writing in my journal. It helps to clear my mind, organize my thoughts, and puts me in the mood to pray.) Dwelling on experiences, thoughts, and blessings that turn our hearts and minds to God paves clean groundwork for prayer. An Elder once told me that he pondered about his blessings to ready himself for prayer. He related: "When I feel I've had a long, hard day and I'm tired and prayer is the last thing on my mind, I just take a few minutes to think about the blessings I received that day and all the things I'm thankful for. I can't help but want to get on my knees and thank the Lord."

The effects of meditation can also be seen in examples from the scriptures. Mosiah 25 cites a case wherein the people were thinking about how the Lord had delivered Alma's people from the Lamanite bondage in the city of Helam. Verse 10 describes the natural outgrowth of their thoughts. "When they thought of the immediate goodness of God, and his power in delivering Alma and his brethren out of the hands of the Lamanites and of bondage, they did raise their voices and give thanks to God."

Pondering is exactly what President Joseph F. Smith was doing when he was given the vision of the redemption of the dead: "I sat in my room pondering over the scriptures; . . . As I pondered over these things which are written, the eyes of my understanding were opened, and the Spirit of the Lord rested upon me." (D&C 138:1, 11.)

This is also what Joseph Smith and Sidney Rigdon were doing as the vision of the three degrees of glory was received. "And while we meditated upon these things, the Lord touched the eyes of our understandings and they were opened, and the glory of the Lord shone around about." (D&C 76:19.) In 1 Nephi 11:1 we read about Nephi's great vision of the tree of life. Note in verse 1 that Nephi mentions he too had been pondering previous to the opening of the vision. These verses demonstrate that pondering is a constructive part of preparation for prayer.

DESIRE TO COMMUNICATE

Among the most important preparations is a genuine desire to communicate. In fact, desire is so essential that it could be termed the cornerstone of preparation. Nephi emphasized the importance of desire when he explained that it was his desire to know the mysteries of God which caused him to cry unto the Lord. (See 1 Nephi 2:16.) The contribution of genuine desire is also illustrated by Enos. He tells us that it was his desire for the welfare of his brethren that brought him to his knees to pour out his whole soul unto God. (See Enos 1:9.) As we build the cornerstone of desire, we too can communicate with God.

SCRIPTURE STUDY

Scripture study is another structural support for prayer. Arthur Bassett explains how this preparation works. "Scripture reading draws us away from the world into the realm of the things of God and supplies a focal point for our meditation. . . . Contemplation of the messages found in the scriptures often provides a good preface to prayer." ("Before Praying," *Ensign*, Jan. 1976, p. 34.) Elder Marion D. Hanks states: "As we read the scriptures, [we] receive the Spirit of the Lord. . . . [This] will help us to want to pray and lead us to experience prayer." (*Prayer*, Deseret Book Co., 1977, p. 28.) I find it beneficial to engage in daily scripture study just prior to prayer because it puts me in a spiritual frame of mind.

Scripture study can also be a means through which the Lord reveals answers to prayer. Sometimes the Lord may choose to respond to an inquiry by bringing a scripture to mind. But he cannot cause us to reflect on a scripture that we have never studied.

HOMEWORK

Another important understructure for a specific answer to prayer is the "homework" step. One of the best illustrations of the homework step is witnessed in Oliver Cowdery's experience during the translation of the Book of Mormon. While acting as a scribe for the Prophet Joseph Smith, Oliver desired to translate and petitioned the Lord to bless him with that gift. Yet when

Oliver tried to do the work of translation, he could not. The Lord then explained that when a gift is desired from him, it is not enough just to ask for it. First we must study it out in our minds; or in other words, we must do our homework.

I suggest this homework consists of checking out the alternatives, weighing values and consequences, considering objectives, in this way preparing a decision to take to the Lord for approval. Oliver had desired a gift; but because he had not done his homework, the Lord could not grant his desire. It is crucial to emphasize the point that although desire is important to prayer, it is not enough. The Lord will not do for us that which we are obligated to do for ourselves. His doing so would deprive us of the opportunity to grow through experience, which is one of the main purposes of earth life. Therefore, doing our homework is an essential step in preparation for making a special request in prayer.

PREPARING TO HEAR

This leads to another foundational basis for prayer: preparing ourselves to hear and accept what the Lord wants to reveal to us. "Be thou humble"; he tells us, "and the Lord thy God shall lead thee by the hand, and give thee answers to thy prayers." (D&C 112:10.) I suggest this can mean that if we are humble, the Lord will lead us to the answer he wants to give to our prayers. While actively seeking to present our "homework" before the Lord, we must humbly allow ourselves to be receptive to the Lord's will. Although the homework step is essential, it does not take precedence over the will of the Lord. Asking for personal revelation from the Lord must include the humility to set aside our own desires if they are contrary to the Lord's will.

FASTING

Fasting is perhaps the most constructive form of preparation. Arthur Bassett explains: "Fasting helps release us somewhat from this world. It helps us recognize our dependence upon the Lord.

It helps demonstrate the seriousness of our intent, both to ourselves and to the Lord. It is a first step in subjecting our will to his. Properly entered into, fasting helps increase our powers of concentration." ("Before Praying," p. 33.)

The scriptures contain many examples of miraculous results produced by fasting used in connection with prayer. It was through fasting and prayer that the sons of Mosiah were able to bring thousands of Lamanites to a knowledge of the gospel. (See Alma 17:3.) This same combination used by Alma the older brought strength to his son's body and a repentant spirit to his soul. (See Mosiah 27:22-23.) With fasting and prayer Christ made his final preparations in the wilderness for starting his formal ministry. (See Luke 4.)

These preparations—obtaining a genuine desire, studying the scriptures, pondering, doing the homework, accepting the Lord's will, and fasting—form a steady, firm foundation for prayer. They build an open, receptive heart that allows us to receive the Spirit which is present in the two-way communication of prayer and personal revelation.

The idea that man can speak with God, the Creator and power of the universe, is boggling to the mind, yet he has commanded us to approach him often. Unlike speaking with great men on the earth, speaking with God requires no official appointment or special position. This privilege is offered to all. President Spencer W. Kimball tells us, "There is a knowledge that our Father in Heaven wants each of us to have, and that is a personal knowledge that he hears and answers our prayers." ("Pray Always," p. 3.)

WE CALL HIM FATHER

As we begin our prayer a marvelous truth is laid before us. Of all the titles applicable to God, he has asked that when we approach him in prayer we call him Father. Perhaps the word *father* conveys his desire to have a personal relationship with each of us, his children. As we commence our prayer with the endearing words *Our Father,* we too suggest our wish to be close to him.

Our Father is interested in all our activities that affect our eternal welfare. He pleads with us to come to him often in prayer and wants us to remember him throughout each day. He lovingly counsels us to "pray always." Figuratively speaking, his arms are outstretched to us in hope that we will reach out for him. We must bear in mind, however, that his respect for our free agency allows him to extend his arms only so far. Therefore, it is essential that we beckon him to be a part of our lives. It is our responsibility to open the door to him by living a life which will invite him to enter.

THE HOLY SPIRIT

As we formally address our Heavenly Father we need to be aware of the factors that influence our capacity to communicate. The most significant of these is the presence of the Holy Spirit. Obtaining that Spirit is an indispensable element in experiencing two-way communication with the Father, since it is the vehicle through which we understand the Father's message to us. This Spirit, then, is a key factor in receiving personal revelation.

An analogy will help demonstrate the role which the Holy Spirit plays in the communication process. Each day the television networks broadcast waves throughout the world. Although these waves are all around us, they cannot be detected or understood without the presence of a receiver, the television set. Similarly, when we pray for personal revelation, the Lord will transmit an answer. He has promised to do so. If our receiver is defective or weak, however, the signal as received will contain much static and interference. Furthermore, if we don't have the receiver at all, we will totally miss the signal. Regardless of how important the message is, the broadcasting waves remain useless without the TV set. Likewise, the Lord's revelations, no matter how vital, cannot be detected by those who lack the Spirit.

To take this analogy one step further, the broadcasting waves are best received on a keenly adjusted, sophisticated instrument. The Spirit is most clearly understood as we become finely tuned and sensitive to its promptings. Since acquiring the Spirit is essential to successful prayer, let's discuss a crucial point which determines the Spirit's presence.

We invite the Spirit to dwell with us throughout the day by living a Christlike life. It is critical for us to understand that if we are not striving daily to follow Christ's example, then the Spirit will not abide with us, thus stunting our attempts at effective two-way communication. The purpose of preparing for prayer, as discussed in the previous chapter, is to invoke the Spirit and get ready to talk with God. Obviously if our lives have knowingly deviated from gospel principles, a sporadic shot at scripture reading or fasting may prove less effective in spiritually preparing us to approach God. This is not to say we should cease to pray when in the midst of sin or depression, rather it is to bring us to the realization that when we are in that lower state it is more difficult if not impossible to receive the Spirit in suffi- cient measure to experience successful prayer.

For example, some years ago I came to a point at which I knew my life needed some reform. By outward appearances I probably gave the impression of being a "good Mormon" — I was going to church, fulfilling my callings, and offering my prayers. Yet I knew inwardly that my private life was past due on an overhaul. A few days after coming to this determination I went camping with some friends. Finding myself in natural outdoor surroundings, I decided to spend some time seeking the Lord in prayer.

I left camp to be on my own. As I began to open up my feelings to the Lord, I must have had Enos's experience in the back of my mind because I really expected to receive some type of impression, voice, or emotion. Instead, I sensed absolutely nothing. I stayed there an hour or two explaining to the Lord that I wanted to repent and asking for some type of acknowledg- ment that he would grant my plea. Still nothing. Finally, I told him that I did not blame him for not answering and just asked for help that I might become more worthy to talk to him.

A few months later I again found myself hiking in the woods.

The passage of time had given me a chance to work out my repentance and had allowed the needed reforms to take positive effect in my life so that the Spirit could dwell with me. Again my desires to communicate with God were aroused, and I sought him in prayer. This time, however, I had the influence of the Holy Ghost with me as I prayed. During my prayer I felt that God was listening. I sensed a closeness to him and an inner swelling of his love. As I wandered back, contemplating what had taken place, I was reminded of my prayer experience of a few months before. I then realized that the difference resulted from my efforts to live a Christlike life which invited the Spirit to dwell with me. I also realized that if I expected to communicate with God and to receive personal revelation in return, it was imperative that I strive daily to follow Christ's teachings and example.

As we experience successful prayer each day, our desire and ability to live a Christlike life will increase. Each is expanded by the other. Prayer should serve as a peak event to enhance our day. It should draw us out of the world for a few minutes so that with our Father's love, strength, and motivation we may prepare ourselves to meet the day's activities.

Expressing Gratitude *Chapter 3*

In sacrament meeting the Sunday before Thanksgiving a speaker related the following experience. "I am the Scoutmaster in my ward. One of my goals is to take my Scouts out once a month on a camp-out. The boys in my troop are fine young men," he went on to commend, "I have never heard them cuss or tell a dirty joke."

He then paused to disclose: "I must tell you something about myself. I really covet my Saturdays. Saturday is the only day I have to spend at home with my family. To give even one of them up is a real sacrifice for me. But I don't mind giving them up to be with these boys." Then he made a sad observation, "There is something that disturbs me, though, and that is that not one of these boys has ever come up and said thank you to me for the sacrifice I have made. They seem to expect it of me. If they would just say those two words, it would make my sacrifice seem so much more worthwhile."

I was so struck by this story that I began to reflect on my own life. I wondered: How many times had I been neglectful of this obligation to say thank you to those who had sacrificed for me?

GIVE THANKS TO GOD

Many of the blessings God gives us are offered to most of us without price. Health, family, happiness, and food become so commonplace that we often take them for granted. Unless we make a conscious effort to be mindful of these blessings, we just seem to expect that they will be there.

One of the greatest opportunities prayer affords us is the privilege to personally express our gratitude to God for the limitless blessings he bestows upon us. Perhaps the Psalmist, more than any other author of scripture, is the greatest example of one who loves to shout praises to the Lord. "I will extol thee, my God, O king; and I will bless thy name for ever and ever. Every day will I bless thee; and I will praise thy name for ever and ever. Great is the Lord, and greatly to be praised." (Psalm 145: 1-3.) He further exhorts all mankind to do the same: "Praise ye the Lord. Praise ye the name of the Lord. . . . Ye that stand in the house of the Lord, in the courts of the house of our God, Praise the Lord; for the Lord is good: sing praises unto his name; for it is pleasant." (Psalm 135:1-3.)

It must be pleasant and perhaps even delightful to God to hear us voice words of praise to him. The Lord expresses his desire for us to share our emotions of thanksgiving with him. "If thou art merry, praise the Lord with singing, with music, with dancing, and with a prayer of praise and thanksgiving." (D&C 136:28.)

King Benjamin reminds us of the depth of our obligation: "O how you ought to thank your heavenly King! . . . you should render all the thanks and praise which your whole soul has power to possess, to that God who has created you, and has kept and preserved you, and has caused that ye should rejoice, and has granted that ye should live in peace one with another." He continues to point out: ". . . He hath created you, and granted unto you your lives, for which ye are indebted unto Him. . . . For behold, are we not all beggars? Do we not all depend upon the same Being, even God, for all the substance which we have, for both food and raiment, and for gold, and for silver and for all the riches which we have of every kind?" (Mosiah 2:19, 20, 23; 4:19.) As King Benjamin has so emphatically stated, we truly are beggars. Literally all we are and possess comes to us by the grace of God.

BE EAGER TO THANK HIM

Considering the endless blessings that are freely showered upon us each day, we should be anxious for the occasion to thank God. Yet too often our eagerness to have the Lord recognize our needs, wants, and desires causes us to dutifully rush through that obligation. Sometimes we eliminate it altogether. No matter what the reason nor how awesome the task may appear, we cannot excuse ourselves from the responsibility of returning thanks to God.

Let us not ignorantly assume that the Lord is not aware whether or not we have filled this responsibility. He is conscious of the blessings he gives us as well as our degree of earnestness to acknowledge them. As Christ journeyed into a village he was approached by ten lepers who pleaded to be healed. Christ told the men to show themselves to the priests. As they went they were miraculously cleansed. Only one returned to give thanks to the Lord. Noting this, Christ questioned: "Were there not ten cleansed? but where are the nine?" (Luke 17:19.) Repeatedly man has been guilty of the sin of the nine lepers, that of ingratitude.

Frequently our prayers lack a conscious effort until we desire a blessing. And too often the major theme of prayer is that of telling the Lord about what we want. I recall an occasion when, after we had moved, my husband was in need of work. He was faithfully going out on a daily job hunt, and I was faithfully engaging in a daily "needs" prayer. Although we had received many recent blessings, such as my husband's graduation from Brigham Young University, a new son, and nice home to live in,

I still caught myself spending less and less time on "thank yous" and more and more time on needs. I've found that returning thanks is not an inherent part of man's character most of the time. Thus, there is a need to learn to shake off the natural man and to make a conscious effort to express gratitude.

MAINTAIN FERVOR IN PRAYERS

In addition to illustrating a laxity in my being thankful, this experience also serves to bring out another tendency that I continually have to guard against. During the time that my husband was without work, my urgency to receive the Lord's help motivated me to pray with great fervor many times each day. After he was offered a job and my initial thanks to God was completed, however, I noticed that the intensity of my prayers diminished. I was inclined to seek the Lord more diligently when facing a problem or crisis.

I suggest that among the many reasons why we find ourselves faced with problems and trials is this tendency to be passive in expressing thanks to God. (I stress that this is only one of many reasons for trials.) Man's inclination during prosperous times is to take lightly his responsibility to thank God with a full heart and real intensity. Therefore, the Lord may allow us to pass through trials because they create an inner distress that causes us to seek help from a divine source.

At a fireside on prayer I attended, the speaker, a returned missionary, shared a personal experience that illustrates how trials motivated him to draw closer to God. He relates: "Previous to my mission my prayers lasted about a minute. They consisted of: Heavenly Father; we thank thee; we ask thee; in the name of Jesus Christ, amen. I put the most effort into my prayers just before a basketball game." A few weeks prior to his leaving on his mission, his mother became ill and had to be hospitalized. "My prayers became really important to me," he said. "For the first time I had a great desire to commune with God." A few days after his mother had been released from the hospital, his father became ill and had to go in. Again the young man was on his knees pleading for the health of his dad. In looking back on the experience, he concluded: "All this aided my mission preparation by putting me in a situation in which I was forced to pray. This helped me to come to know God better." Trials do help us to come to a realization of the extent of our dependency on God and consequently to strengthen our relationship with him.

SEEK GOD EARLY IN THANKFULNESS

Of even greater value and beauty is a relationship with God that has been built out of sincere praise and adoration. I believe the Lord gave us the formula to develop this type of relationship when he counseled: "Those that seek me early shall find me." (Proverbs 8:17.) In other words, we must seek to make thanksgiving our initiative to find him before our lives are crippled with trials and we are compelled by despair. Prayer need not be a resounding siren for the Lord to lift our yokes or ease our burdens. Rather it can be a constant relationship prepared early in times of prosperity and depended upon in times of famine.

One of the greatest examples of this kind of thankful prayer is in the life of my mother. I recall that on many occasions after she had arrived home from an event or meeting in which she had participated or had been in charge she would excuse herself, go to her bedroom, and give thanks for the divine help which had been manifest. If I or one of my brothers or sister had been involved, she would invite us to come with her. When our family had been the recipient of a special blessing, she was quick to point it out and to remind us of our responsibility to express appreciation to the Lord.

By taking every opportunity to formally thank our Father for his kindness, we will develop a grateful attitude. Developing this attitude will cause us to rise to higher levels of prayer. This happens because as we thank the Lord, he will acknowledge our expressions by bestowing further blessings upon us. The Lord promises us that "he who receiveth all things with thankfulness shall be made glorious; and the things of this earth shall be added unto him, even an hundred fold, yea more." (D&C 78:19.) The continuing flow of blessings will stimulate our desire to kneel in prayer more often. Thus, thanksgiving will build our relationship with God.

One of the most beneficial suggestions I ever received was from a talk given in church. A young lady challenged us to a prayer of thanksgiving. We were instructed that in this prayer there were to be no requests made; rather our total intent was to thank God for our numerous blessings. I took her challenge to heart. After trying it, I felt so good inside and had such a richer relationship with our Father that I set a goal to engage in this type of prayer at least once a week.

As we express gratitude to our Father for his eternal generosity to us, the failing exhibited by the nine lepers becomes absent from our lives and we prepare for eternal life by coming to know God. Clearly the faithful servant is compelled to his knees in fervent prayer by an overwhelming realization of the greatness and richness of his blessings. He is drawing nearer to God.

Nurturing the Spirit

The spring after our wedding my husband and I decided to follow the prophet's counsel to plant a garden. After a few seminars we felt somewhat more confident that, in spite of our "Caucasian thumbs," we would later be picking ears of corn off a plant rather than off the vegetable counter at the local supermarket. So in family home evening we made a plan to prepare the ground with fertilizer and to plant a variety of vegetables.

We were excited as we shoveled and plowed the soil and then one by one planted the seeds. The excitement soon wore off, however, as we realized that after a hard day of working away from home, we still had to face pulling weeds and watering plants. Worse yet, activities such as staking tomatoes and thinning beets began depriving us of some precious Saturday TV and racquetball time. Needless to say, this period of nurturing and cultivating taxed every ounce of our self-discipline. Still, we knew that if the gardening was not done properly, the garden's growth would be stunted and our harvest would yield weeds instead of vegetables.

A wise gardener realizes that just planting the seeds is not enough. An abundant harvest necessitates a season of cultivation and growth. Likewise the spiritual seeds of preparation we plant before prayer also require a time of nurturing during prayer. In this time we nurture an inner growth of the Holy Spirit to prepare us for listening and understanding God's communication to us. Just as a careless gardener forfeits an abundant high-quality crop, so by neglecting to cultivate the Spirit properly we sacrifice the harvest of two-way communication with God.

Perhaps you may be questioning: What does it mean to nurture the Spirit? How does nurturing the Spirit affect my ability to receive communication? How is the Spirit nurtured during prayer?

EXPRESSING GRATITUDE NURTURES THE SPIRIT

No one can dispute the *need* to have a garden. The *how* of gardening is somewhat more elusive. The same is true in the relationship between expressing gratitude and nurturing the Spirit. In the previous chapter we established the need to express gratitude. In this chapter we will explore how to nurture the Spirit through the principle of expressing gratitude.

When we do it properly, expressing gratitude is a tool we can use to increase our capacity to receive the Spirit and to make us sensitive to its prompting. The purpose of our thanking the Lord for our blessings is not only to express gratitude but also to help us nurture the Spirit to a degree that we become attuned to personal revelation.

Consider the spiritual swelling you experience in a testimony meeting. This swelling is a product of edifying one another through sharing spiritual insights, bearing testimonies, and expressing gratitude for blessings. Because the law of edification has been observed, we all rejoice together and the Spirit abounds. (See D&C 50:22.) By applying this principle to prayer through sharing our testimonies and our insights, and most importantly, expressing our thanks to the Lord, we can experience edification. This causes the spiritual growth that maximizes our personal ability to receive and understand the Lord's revelations. President Spencer W. Kimball said: "A wonderful and assuring

spirit comes over us as we express sincere gratitude to Heavenly
Father for our blessings." ("Pray Always," p. 4.)

EDIFICATION THROUGH THANKSGIVING

A key to experiencing edification and thus nurturing the
Spirit during prayer is found in the method used to express
gratitude to the Lord. When used as a step to nurture the Spirit,
thanksgiving must have more self-involvement than just voicing
blessings. Too frequently the procedure is to rattle off a list of
"thank yous" without any feeling for what is being said. State-
ments, such as "I'm thankful for the missionaries," and "I'm
thankful for my family," become trite phrases rather than fervent
praises.

Although we may be sincerely grateful for a blessing, if our
statement of appreciation is not stimulated and supported by our
immediate feelings, we limit our capacity for the Spirit. The
Lord indicates that we must thank him in the Spirit for each
blessing we receive. (D&C 46:32.) In other words, an honest,
heartfelt emotion aroused by a spirit of gratitude must inspire the
words we utter. These feelings must accompany each blessing we
thank God for.

EXPERIENCE THE EMOTIONS, BE SPECIFIC

Perhaps a couple of suggestions can help us achieve this type
of thanksgiving. First, it is essential to be experiencing the
emotions aroused by the blessings at the time the words are
uttered. This can be done by stopping to consider *why* you are
grateful for the blessing before you speak. For example, in being
thankful for the prophet you may ponder his message in the
previous conference, considering how it has helped you or
caused a change in your life. In expressing thankfulness for
parents you may think about a recent gift of love or time they
gave in your behalf. The feelings that arise from these reflections

will prick the heart so that the words uttered will be generated by the emotions of the soul.

Second, be specific in your expressions. Tell the Lord why you appreciate the gift or kindness he has shown you. Following this process of your pondering each blessing before acknowledging it to the Lord will simultaneously cause the desired nurturing of the Spirit that prepares you to detect and comprehend the Lord's communication to you.

It was as I entered college life that I first stumbled onto the effect expressing gratitude can have on prayer. Before I left home I knew that I would be facing many challenges. Paramount in my mind was my monetary situation. I knew I had to find a job soon if I was to meet my financial obligations. This, coupled with all the other anxieties (such as roommates and classes) that accompany a freshman to college, motivated me to turn to the Lord in prayer for help.

Upon arrival at my dorm, I received my first interview with my dorm mother prior to my room assignment. By the end of the interview she had offered me a job at the dorm as a resident assistant. I was also able to get the classes I needed at the times I wanted them. Most surprising of all is that I found a roommate who I could get along with and even enjoy.

The Sunday before classes started, while writing in my journal I began to ponder over how everything had fallen into place so easily. As I pondered I realized that God had answered my prayers and had taken care of me. I had a sense of security and knew he really loved me. As I meditated I felt a great urgency to express my gratitude to my Father in prayer. I thanked him over and over for showing me such kindness. The emotions which swelled out of these expressions created a desire to further thank him for other blessings. As I pursued this desire and continued to share my appreciation, I felt very close to Heavenly Father. The Spirit seemed to grow with each word of gratitude.

It was then that I began to see the natural result of expressing gratitude in a manner that nurtured the Spirit. Pondering about why I was thankful for a blessing before voicing thanks for it caused my words to have personal meaning. Thus, I felt that God was really hearing what I had to say.

EFFECT ON COMMUNICATION

Even more noticeable was the effect that expressing gratitude had on my ability to listen to the personal revelation that God communicated to me. As I reflect on the experience, I remember how easy it was to comprehend the Lord's inspiration to me. The answers to my questions and the solutions to my problems were completely clear. This is the natural outcome of nurturing the Spirit through thanksgiving. At the time I didn't realize what was happening. It wasn't until later with the advantage of more knowledge and hindsight that the impact of this experience came.

Most often this nurturing of the Spirit occurs during prayer. However, there are times when our present thoughts or immediate circumstances create a situation which has caused a great spiritual swelling. On these occasions usually there is an intense inner desire to talk to Heavenly Father. For me, these desires generally occur after an uplifting meeting, as a result of an inspiring conversation, while I am thinking about blessings, or as I am pondering spiritual concepts and ideas. It is exciting to take advantage of these special moments and feelings. They yield the opportunity of true communion because the Spirit is already present in great abundance.

Truman G. Madsen wrote: "Half, at least, of the prayer process is bringing our souls into receptivity so that we may be powerful listeners." ("Prayer and the Prophet Joseph," *Ensign,* Jan. 1976, p. 20.) A major part of prayer is the cultivating period, at which time we make our souls receptive to the Spirit in anticipation of listening to communication from God. Therefore, thanking the Lord has a dual purpose: First, to express gratitude for all the blessings bestowed upon us, and second, to nurture the Spirit to a degree that prepares us for the next part of communication with God, that of receiving personal revelation.

Pondering

The Lord poses a concept that can be somewhat disturbing if we do not understand the process of prayer. He states: "Whatsoever ye ask the Father in my name it shall be given unto you, *that is expedient for you*; And if you ask anything that is not expedient for you, it shall turn unto your condemnation." (D&C 88:64-65; italics added.) Reading this scripture is usually a prologue to the question, How do I know if what I am asking the Lord is, in reality, expedient for me? In a letter to the Romans, Paul opens our minds to some key ideas on this question.

> . . . We know not what we should pray for as we ought: but the Spirit itself maketh intercession for us with groanings which cannot be uttered.
> And he that searcheth the hearts knoweth what is the mind of the Spirit, because he maketh intercession for the saints according to the will of God. (Romans 8:26-27.)

PRAYER CONTENT REVEALED

We can draw from this scripture that we do not always have the foresight to discern what is expedient for us; therefore, the Spirit intercedes and awakens our hearts to what God wills that we ask. In other words, God, through the Spirit, will tell us what is expedient for us to pray for.

The Lord taught this doctrine to Joseph Smith: "But know this, it shall be given you what you shall ask." (D&C 50:30.) Apparently the Nephites also understood this principle. The record of Christ's visit to the Americas cites an instance wherein Christ commands his twelve disciples to pray. Verse 24 of 3 Nephi 19 explains how they knew what to ask: ". . . they did not multiply many words, for it was given unto them what they should pray." Through these scriptures the Lord indicates that the knowledge of what is expedient to ask can come as a direct personal revelation during prayer. As we take steps to receive and cultivate the Spirit to the extent that we are able to hear and understand its promptings, it will communicate to us what God wills us to ask. We receive this knowledge as we ponder and listen.

As with some of the previous steps, pondering to be inspired as to what to ask may be a new concept to many. Traditionally we are taught to say, "Our Heavenly Father, we thank thee . . . ; we ask thee . . . ; in the name of Jesus Christ, amen." Although this approach is good because it is simple and basic, perhaps there are intermediate steps which allow us to understand the principles involved in prayer and to rise to higher levels of communication with God.

INSPIRATION THROUGH PONDERING

It will be helpful to address the question of what process is involved in receiving inspiration. I suggest that after preparing for and beginning prayer, we should dedicate time to meaningful expressions of gratitude assisted by pondering about why we are thankful for a blessing, and then vocalizing that thanks. When the Spirit has been nurtured to a degree that we believe we can discern and understand its promptings, we should then begin pondering. The pondering step will allow the Lord the opportunity to reveal or confirm what he would like us to ask.

The awaited personal revelation usually centers around recent problems, thoughts, and feelings. Most often it is an impression to inquire about the things pondered in the homework step which was done prior to prayer. This is logical because it encourages us to be "anxiously engaged" in doing homework so we may receive the growth this step affords. By pondering, we allow the Lord an opportunity to confirm that he wants to hear the ideas we have "studied out."

PRACTICE TO UNDERSTAND REVELATIONS

Learning to understand these revelations requires practice and experience. I recall some experiences I have had with the pondering process. My husband teaches early morning seminary; therefore I desire to include a prayer for his efforts in this calling each day. As I come to the pondering step I strive to allow the Spirit to inspire the blessing I ask. Often I don't sense any particular influence from the Spirit about what to say—just a confirmation to express my own thoughts and intuitions. Usually these stem from my husband's comments about the lesson and the students. However, sometimes I do feel moved to request a special blessing for my husband that day. Other times I sense a prompting to request that the Lord bless the youth in a particular need. Occasionally I feel that I should pray for an individual in the class.

Here is another example. Each month I prepare for my Relief Society visiting teaching by setting appointments, reading the message, and thinking about each of the sister's needs. The morning of my visits, in my personal prayer I seek the Lord's help in them. Often I have some particular things in mind that I would like the Lord to help me with. When I arrive at the pondering step, I don't just start rattling off a list of requests for help. I wait and ponder in order to allow the Lord an opportunity to influence what I ask. Usually I feel a confirmation to present the ideas that I have planned. This indication can be the sole prompting, or it may be accompanied by others. Occasionally I am moved to ask a different or an additional blessing for a sister. Sometimes I am impressed during the lesson to make a point that I hadn't previously considered.

Many times I do not find out if what I was impressed to say was of any consequence. But on the occasions when the evidences of pondering have been apparent, my testimony of the importance of including this step in prayer has grown. Of great importance is the fact that we please the Lord when we seek his will and desire his influence in our prayers and lives.

ADDITIONAL INSPIRATION

When we are in tune, the Lord may also choose to reveal additional inspiration, prompting us to inquire about events, experiences, or thoughts that we hadn't intended on saying. Sometimes these promptings alert us to events that have already happened, or they prepare us for an experience that will come in the near future.

I recall that once while pondering I received an impression to pray for a friend whom I had not thought about for some time. As a result of that impression I decided to contact her. During a succeeding visit she shared with me deeply felt emotions about her shaky testimony and about a questionable relationship she was considering. I honestly believe that if I had not been pondering and praying that the Lord might inspire my inquiries, this chance to help my friend would have been lost or given to another.

On another occasion I felt prompted to write to my former mission president and his wife. She had developed cancer while serving on their mission. Since completion of their mission, however, she had survived four years. At the time the impression came, I had not communicated with them for some time. Yet as the prompting came I knew that if I didn't write soon she would be gone and I would miss the chance. I wrote and mailed a letter the next day. Two weeks later I received word of her passing.

In developing the skill of pondering, we may not sense promptings in every word we say; but as we seek this level of communication we will feel the promptings of the Spirit with greater frequency. The reason why is that this is a skill. Recognizing inspiration is meant to be a challenging process. And as we are persistent, we will become more susceptible to the Spirit's promptings and will be more successful in our communication efforts.

HOMEWORK PROCESS NECESSARY

A modern example of the Lord's inspiring a prayer is given in Elder Bruce R. McConkie's account of the revelation of the priesthood. He relates:

> On the first day of June . . . 1978, the First Presidency and the Twelve, after full discussion of the proposition and all the premises and principles that are involved, importuned the Lord for a revelation. President Kimball was mouth, and he prayed with great faith and great fervor; this was one of those occasions when an inspired prayer was offered. You know the Doctrine and Covenants statement, that if we pray by the power of the Spirit we will receive answers to our prayers and it will be given us what we shall ask. (D&C 50:30.) It was given President Kimball what he should ask. He prayed by the power of the Spirit, and there was perfect unity, total and complete harmony, between the Presidency and the Twelve on the issue involved. (*Priesthood*, Deseret Book Co., 1981, p. 133.)

As pointed out by Elder McConkie, the Lord inspired President Kimball as to what he should ask. Note that although they awaited the Lord's inspiration to inquire on the matter, they did not consider this an excuse to neglect the homework process.

"Extended meditation and prayer" were an essential prelude to the revelation. (See Official Declaration — 2 in the 1981 edition of the Doctrine and Covenants.) We are not relieved of this obligation by the anticipation of receiving the Lord's mind and will.

"Perfect prayers are those which are inspired, in which the Spirit reveals the words which should be used." (Bruce R. McConkie, *Mormon Doctrine*, Bookcraft, Inc., p. 586.) We can help in this perfecting of our prayers by granting the Lord the freedom to influence our utterings through pondering and awaiting his inspiration as the Spirit teaches us to pray. As we do this, our communications will become more meaningful to ourselves as well as to the Lord. The greatest benefit will be the magnified influence the Lord can have in our lives.

Asking According to Inspiration

Chapter 6

The revelation received during the pondering step supplies the blueprint from which we construct our requests. Because they are the will of God, these revealed blueprints are keys to having our prayers answered. The Lord makes a commitment to those who ask according to his will. Doctrine and Covenants 46:30 states: "He that asketh in the Spirit asketh according to the will of God; wherefore it is done even as he asketh." In my own experience the fundamental components found in a plea that is to be fulfilled are: the Spirit, received during thanksgiving; the revelation of the Lord's will, received during pondering; and the petition, asking in the Spirit according to the revealed will of the Lord.

PETITION SIGNIFIES AN AGREEMENT

It is important to realize the extent of our responsibility when we petition the Lord for a knowledge of what he wills us to ask. As we make that petition, we are simultaneously making a type of agreement. In effect this agreement states that the Lord consents to reveal his plan as long as we structure and conform our prayers and lives in harmony with it. If we choose not to unite our will to the Lord's and not to ask as he directs, we risk our right to be entitled to revelation in the future. Therefore, as we ask that these impressions may penetrate our minds and hearts, we are obligated to make them the blueprint from which we build our requests.

REQUESTS SHOULD ACCORD WITH GOD'S WILL

The Lord explained that not asking in accordance with his will is the reason why many of our prayers are not answered: "Ye ask, and ye receive not, because ye ask amiss." (James 4:3.) He further warned Oliver Cowdery: "Do not ask for that which you ought not." (D&C 8:10.) Many frustrating hours can be avoided by disciplining ourselves to importune the Lord in harmony with his desire and avoiding the temptation to ask amiss.

I had an experience that impressed upon me the inner peace that results from seeking to ask in accordance with God's will. After returning home from my mission, my thoughts naturally turned to my next goals of college and marriage. After pondering and planning I came to some decisions to present to the Lord for approval. In the marriage area I had narrowed my selection to a specific "who." As I left for college in the fall, I knew he would be returning from his mission in a few months. He was scheduled to return at the same time my missionary brother was. When my parents called to ask if I would like to come home for the weekend of my brother's homecoming, I was not only elated at the invitation of seeing my family but also anxious to see if this young man had any feelings for me.

It was a thrilling weekend. The delightful visit I had with my family was only surpassed by the exciting time I had renewing acquaintances with my friend. Needless to say, I looked forward to Christmas vacation with great anticipation. A few nights before I would be going home for the holidays he called. By the end of the conversation I believed that he too was looking forward to my return. The morning of my departure I knelt in prayer. I had studied the situation out in my mind and was ready to present my plan. But as I came to the pondering step, I did not feel a confirmation of the Spirit to ask as I desired. In fact, the only request I felt inspired to utter went something like this: "Father, this young man seems to be interested in me, and I am interested in him. If it is thy will that we marry, bless our relationship to develop while I am home. But if this is not thy will, let everything subside. Please help me to accept what happens."

By the end of the vacation the Lord had undoubtedly given me an answer. Absolutely nothing had happened—not even a phone call. Of course I was hurt by the rejection, but I found comfort in the fact that I knew this was the Lord's will, and I desired to follow it.

A few days after returning to college for winter semester I met Rob. We started dating at the beginning of March. I recall my prayer after our first date. Even before kneeling down, I felt impressed to inquire about our relationship. (I should point out that it wasn't my habit to question the Lord about every man I dated.) Pondering briefly during my prayer, I felt intensely that I should ask about Rob. The Lord's reply came as an overwhelming joy. Through the following weeks the Lord reconfirmed his answer by causing this joy and excitement to grow. When Rob asked me to marry him the next month, there was no question in my mind as to whether the Lord sanctioned our relationship.

These experiences impressed upon me the importance of allowing the Spirit to influence our inquiries. In each case the request I wanted to make was basically the same. The contrast was found in the prompting I received of what God desired me to ask. The first time the Spirit did not suggest that I inquire about marriage. The second time I was impressed with an urge to seek the Lord's blessing upon our relationship. In the first instance with my friend, had I asked what I wanted I may have been disappointed and confused when the Lord did not respond with the answer I expected. Repeated disappointment and confusion could have affected my inner confidence in prayer. Such confusion can sometimes create an ignorant assumption that God doesn't answer prayers.

These experiences build my testimony of the importance of seeking to supplicate the Lord in harmony with his will. A peace attends those who desire to be divinely inspired as to what to say. Our forsaking the temptation to ask amiss allows God the opportunity to respond in accordance with what has been petitioned.

EFFECTS OF ASKING AMISS

Persisting in asking amiss can be detrimental. This is exemplified in Joseph Smith and Martin Harris's experience with losing the 116 manuscript pages of the Book of Mormon. In spite of the Lord's initial denial of Martin Harris's request to take the manuscript to show his wife and friends, Martin and Joseph continued to plead with the Lord to submit to that request. Finally the Lord yielded to their demand. The result was the loss of the manuscript and the heartache and chastening it brought especially to the Prophet.

NO RESPONSE MAY BE ANSWER

We need to recognize that not being moved to inquire about a troubling question may also be regarded as an answer. Depending on the nature of the question, the Lord might be suggesting, "No, don't worry about it," or, "It's not time to know that information."

For example, while teaching at the Missionary Training Center I would occasionally chat with an Elder who had become discouraged with prayer because he had been requesting to know if his present girl friend was "the right one" and felt that the Lord hadn't revealed an answer. Usually the Elder would be surprised to realize that the Lord's "no response" was the unrecognized answer. The Lord knew it wasn't the appropriate time for the young man to receive the specific information he sought. Had the Elder included the pondering step in his prayers, he may have perceived the Lord's decision and avoided the anxiety.

"ACCORDING TO THY WORD"

As our ability to live by and pray with the Spirit matures, we can become so in tune with the Lord that our actions and desires are one with his. The prophet Nephi who lived during the time of the preparation for the visit of Christ to the Americas is perhaps one of the finest examples of a man who had mastered the ability of asking and living according to the Lord's will. He became so proficient in this skill that the Lord granted him this supreme promise:

> Blessed art thou, Nephi, for those things which thou hast done; for I have beheld how thou hast with unwearyingness declared the word, which I have given unto thee, unto this people. And thou hast not feared them, and hast not sought thine own life, but hast sought my will, and to keep my commandments.
>
> And now, because thou hast done this with such unwearyingness, behold, I will bless thee forever; and I will make thee mighty in word and in deed, in faith and in works; yea, even that all things shall be done unto thee according to thy word, for thou shalt not ask that which is contrary to my will. (Helaman 10:4-5.)

What a compliment to the prophet Nephi! The Lord trusted him so much that he could make this promise to him. Nephi had earned the Lord's trust through demonstrating an undeviating pursuit for knowledge of the Lord's will and then designing and living his life accordingly.

In the workshop of prayer we can develop the skill of pondering to discover the Lord's plan and then construct our inquiries in unison with it. By proving our competence in this skill, we can have Nephi's promise extended to us. We too can be trusted of the Lord.

Listening: Mistakes and Misunderstandings

The story is told of a telegraph operator in the early part of this century who was looking for employment. Arriving at an office in response to a help-wanted ad, he was ushered into a room with about ten other applicants.

As he sat there he overheard various conversations around the room. He noted that most of the applicants seemed to be preoccupied with comparing their notable qualifications and flaunting their infinite hours of experience.

Suddenly the man jumped up and ran into the employer's office. Within a few minutes he emerged with a confident smile and left. The secretary then excused the remaining applicants, explaining that the position had been taken. Filled with dismay, they filed out of the office. One hurriedly caught up with the man and asked why he got the job while the others didn't even get an interview. The new employee replied, with a questioning look, "Didn't you hear the morse code message announcing that the first person to come into the employer's office would be hired?"

A close examination of this story may be beneficial in helping us discover some of the mistakes and misunderstandings that hinder the listening process in prayer. First, the unwanted applicants were not disqualified by insufficient knowledge or skill.

They were deprived of the position by their failure to apply their knowledge and skill at the appropriate time. Each had become so obsessed with explaining and evaluating his own abilities and comparing them against the qualifications of others in the room that all were oblivious to the most important instruction.

The application is obvious: In striving to establish two-way communication with God we must not become so busy diagnosing our personal circumstances and seeking the advice of others that we fail to ask and listen for God's vital instructions to us. We need to discipline ourselves and demonstrate our knowledge and desire to hear the Lord's will by listening carefully for his directions.

We can draw another principle from this story. Let's suppose that a person with no knowledge of the telegraph code had been present in the room. Because he was unskilled, he would have missed the message even if he had been listening. In our communication with God we must acquire the necessary knowledge and skills as well as the ability to apply them.

A scriptural example gives further illustration. At the time Jesus Christ appeared to the ancient inhabitants of the Americas, the Father introduced his Son three times. While they all heard the voice, "they understood it not." The third time they comprehended the Father's words. (See 3 Nephi 11:3-7.) It seems that the voice did not get louder or clearer with each utterance, but that the change which permitted the multitude to grasp the message was that they "did open their ears to hear." In other words, each person had to spiritually attune himself in order to hear and understand. This experience of the ancient inhabitants demonstrates that the Lord can be sending communications to us and yet we can be completely ignorant of the message. Just as these people had to develop the ability to listen and discern the Lord's communication through the Spirit, so must we if we expect to detect and understand the answers the Lord reveals to our prayers.

Yet as we strive to develop this skill, we occasionally become discouraged. We have faith in God's promises to hear and answer all our prayers, but we lack the confident feeling and knowledge that accompanies revelation. Sometimes we don't seem to perceive any indication of divine guidance. Other times we feel confused and we are not sure of what is being said. Let's analyze some reasons why we have difficulty in perceiving inspiration.

WHY WE DO NOT DETECT OR RECEIVE ANSWERS

SIN

Perhaps the most obvious reason for not comprehending God's counsel is that our power of discernment has become calloused by sin. Nephi explained this to Laman and Lemuel.

> Ye are swift to do iniquity but slow to remember the Lord your God. Ye have seen an angel, and he spake unto you; yea, ye have heard his voice from time to time; and he hath spoken unto you in a still small voice, but ye were past feeling, that ye could not feel his words. (1 Nephi 17:45.)

As clarified by the prophet Nephi, iniquity caused his brothers to be "past feeling," to be unable to feel the Lord's revelations as revealed through the still small voice.

Our sins don't have to be as serious as Laman's and Lemuel's to affect our ability to grasp the Lord's messages. Any deviation from the straight and narrow path will decrease our spiritual sensitivity, and will thus blunt the interpretive tool needed for discerning revelation.

SPIRITUAL PREPARATION

We have discussed previously the need for spiritual preparation, such as scripture study, and also pondering done just previous to prayer. Failure to prepare our minds and hearts with the Spirit prior to prayer is another factor that will impair our ability to receive and understand the Lord's messages. On the first day of his ministry in ancient America, Christ recognized that the people were lacking in this area of preparation:

> I perceive that ye are weak, that ye cannot understand all my words which I am commanded of the Father to speak unto you at this time.
>
> Therefore, go ye unto your homes, and ponder upon the things which I have said, and ask of the Father in my name, that ye may understand, and prepare your minds for the morrow, and I come unto you again. (3 Nephi 17:2-3.)

Although these people who had been spared from the destruction at the time of the Crucifixion were the more righteous, Christ perceived that still they were not totally prepared spiritually to receive his message. Hence, he counseled them to go home, ponder and pray about what he had told them, and prepare their minds for the next day's instruction. This suggests that being honest in heart is not enough. They needed a further spiritual preparation if they were to understand fully the teachings Christ had given and would give them. In addition to living righteously, we too need to prepare spiritually before prayer.

HOMEWORK NOT DONE

While unrighteousness and spiritual unpreparedness diminish our ability to receive and understand the Lord's promptings, his apparent silence may lead us to believe that he has not heard or not answered our prayers, whereas in actuality it is we who are at fault—we have become insensitive to the Spirit. Certain other conditions may cause the Lord to choose not to actively respond to our petitions or may diminish the clarity of the message received.

One such condition is our failure to do our "homework" (see chapter 1). The purpose of our earthly existence would be defeated if God were to solve all our problems before giving us a chance to discover solutions ourselves. As an analogy, while working as a teacher's aide in an elementary school I was asked to help a boy who was having trouble in reading. He had not learned to sound out words. When he would get stuck on a word I would have him try to figure it out to the best of his ability and then I would tell him if he was correct. As his competence at sounding out words grew, his reading skills improved. Had I always told him the words, he never would have acquired this skill and thus would have remained handicapped in reading.

Obviously, as we become proficient in studying out situations in our minds, weighing values and alternatives, and presenting a decision to the Lord, we grow in knowledge and intelligence and advance toward godhood. The Lord's refusal to respond to our pleas for him to make decisions and plans for us demonstrates his knowledge of and respect for the perfecting process that is designed to return us to him.

The story of the brother of Jared attests to the increased knowledge and intensified faith that comes from doing one's homework. As the Jaredites were preparing the barges to journey to the promised land they became aware of two major problems. The barges didn't allow for air or light. The brother of Jared went to the Lord to ask what they should do. The Lord revealed the solution to provide air for the barge. He explained, "Thou shalt make a hole in the top, and also in the bottom; and when thou shalt suffer for air thou shalt unstop the hole and receive air." (Ether 2:20.) After carrying out the Lord's instructions, the brother of Jared returned to inquire what they should do to provide light in the barges. Instead of solving the problem this time, the Lord questioned: "What will ye that I should prepare for you that ye may have light when ye are swallowed up in the depths of the sea?" (Ether 2:25.) In response to the Lord's challenge the brother of Jared devised a plan. He prepared sixteen stones to present to the Lord—he had faith that they would be illuminated if the Lord would touch them. And they were. Moreover, the record seems to indicate that as he worked on this plan his knowledge and faith increased, so that when he returned to present it to the Lord he could not be kept without the veil, and he saw Christ.

When we assume our homework responsibility, we too open the door which permits God to answer our prayers, and additionally we experience the related inner growth. God will not relieve us of this obligation to ourselves and to our future, for this process enables us to become like him. If we plead for him to relieve us of our agency, he wisely waits until we realize the need to assume our task first.

I must point out that in the homework process there is still a need to be openly listening for inspiration. Often the Lord may have some counsel to give us on the situation that we will miss if we are totally self-reliant. There is a delicate balance between the extremes of (1) total self-reliance and (2) complete dependence on God in the name of faith. The fact is that success on different occasions may require different proportions of each.

A good friend shared this story with me. While serving as a Primary president she was asked to be in charge of the Christmas program. She recalled: "I tried very hard to put together a nice program. I even fasted and prayed. But the program was a total flop. The tape recorder didn't work, I forgot my lines, and Santa was late." She sadly admitted, "I don't understand why the Lord let me down. I did all I could."

As we discussed the incident, some interesting facts came out. I questioned: "After you had fasted and prayed, did you ask the Lord if there was anything else you needed to be aware of to make the program a success? Did you listen for further guidance?" To these questions she replied, "No, I never considered that. I thought that after I had done my part I would fast and pray and leave it in the hands of the Lord."

This experience can teach us a valuable lesson. If my friend had been listening, perhaps the Lord would have guided her to have another tape recorder on hand or to check up on the Santa committee. While one of the purposes of fasting and prayer is to demonstrate faith in the Lord, sometimes that same faith should require of us more action than just "leaving it in the Lord's hands." We ought not to assume that we are not entitled to God's guidance during the homework process, or that after we have completed what we consider our portion of the homework our task is done and God does not have more inspiration for us. Needless to say, we had better not assume that God will perform a miracle, great or small, that we could have performed ourselves if we had been listening.

Thus we see that the homework process calls for a balance between total self-reliance and total dependence on God. Not seeking that balance can lead again to the frustrating experience of feeling that our prayers have not been answered.

INDECISIVENESS

A tendency to indecisiveness also keeps us from receiving a confirmation of the Spirit. A lawyer once related this experience to me. After being with an established law firm for some time, he wanted to open his own office. As he considered the risks of being on his own, however, fear would keep him from making the final commitment. He described how he would plead for the Lord to help him make up his mind, yet the communication lines seemed barricaded.

One day his employer called him in to discuss plans for the coming year. He knew the time had come. He had to choose between staying on or leaving the firm. Still the Lord would not answer his desperate pleas. Upon arrival at work the next morning he noticed his employer was free and felt impressed to walk into his office.

"The words just came out of my mouth." he explained. "As soon as I announced that I was leaving the firm, the confirmation of the Spirit just burned inside me. Everything began to fall into place. Within two hours I had a new office location. Some friends offered the necessary financial support, and I was able to buy most of my office furniture at a discount price."

This story evidences the Lord's desire for us to learn to evaluate alternatives, consequences, and values, and with our own wisdom to make a decision to take to him for confirmation.

LEARNING EXPERIENCE

At times the Lord uses our experiences as workshops to teach us a principle or to mold us with a character trait we'll need for meeting future challenges. I recall that after having been out of high school a few years, my girl friend and I had an urge to try apartment living. We chose a town quite a few miles from home and began to make plans to move. I felt that a decision as monumental as moving out on my own should have the Lord's approval, so I asked him to tell me if this was the right thing for me to do. When I didn't receive any recognizable impression, I decided to go ahead as planned. I reasoned that if God didn't care enough to tell me his will one way or another, I would do as I pleased.

In retrospect I know that moving was the right decision, but my conclusion as to why the Lord didn't answer my prayer was wrong. I realize that God was trying to teach me the principle of self-reliance. Had he revealed that it was his desire that I move, I may not have had the necessary self-determination to make the situation work. I probably would have been more apt to rely on God to cause things to fall into place. The Lord knew that I needed to learn the value and use of self-reliance because it would be a vital tool in the coming years of my life.

ALL OPTIONS SATISFACTORY

Occasionally the Lord doesn't reply, because all the choices we have presented to him are acceptable. In other words, it doesn't matter to him which we choose; any alternative is satisfactory. This situation is recorded several times in the Doctrine and Covenants. For example, in section 60, the elders who had been appointed to return to the East to do missionary work were desiring to know how they should proceed. Specifically they wanted to know whether to make or buy a craft for the journey. In verse five the Lord tells them that it doesn't matter to him: "Let there be a craft made, or bought, as seemeth you good; it mattereth not unto me."

In a sacrament meeting I once heard a sister relate a relevant personal experience. Her family had recently moved from another city, and they were trying to find a suitable place to live. They narrowed their decision to three homes and sought guidance from the Lord as to which house would be the best for their family. The Lord responded with a negative answer about one house, yet they sensed no definite answer over the remaining two. In spite of their constant efforts to seek the Lord's will, nothing seemed to come. Finally they decided to choose of their own accord. Shortly after the family moved in, her husband was called to be the bishop of the ward. As they reflected over their experience, they realized that the home they were not to buy was outside the ward boundaries, while the other two were not. Clearly, as long as they were in this ward's boundaries it didn't matter to the Lord where they lived. These examples help us to understand that there are times when any option we select will please the Lord. We grow by using our own discretion to make a choice.

Prior to the discussion on the actual listening (see next chapter), here is a summary of the points discussed above:

1. Unrighteousness callouses our power to discern, consequently we are "past feeling" the Spirit.
2. Spiritual unpreparedness produces an insensitivity to the Spirit.
3. Failure to complete our homework may be the reason why we have not received an answer.
4. The Spirit withholds confirmation until we have reached a final decision we can submit.
5. The potential growth experience is of great value, so the Lord frequently does not respond immediately.

6. We may receive no specific answer because all the alternatives are satisfactory, and we are to choose of our own accord.

As we become aware of some of the reasons why we may not receive or perceive revelation, we will feel less frustrations when our prayer efforts seem futile.

Listening:
A Developed Skill

T he training for my mission included many technique classes. On one occasion I was asked to be the investigator in a role-playing exercise which was to demonstrate the importance of testimony. As the sisters who were teaching me completed their testimony of the Book of Mormon, I questioned, "How do you know it is true?" One of the sisters replied, "Because I have a burning in my bosom?" Then I further probed, "What is a burning in the bosom?"

As I asked that question I changed roles from a role-playing investigator to a lifetime member of the Church. I really wanted to know what a burning in the bosom felt like. Often I had waited in vain for that feeling while searching for an answer to prayers I had offered the Lord.

This can be a perplexing problem. It is discouraging when we don't perceive any type of inspiration or answer to our prayer or when we don't understand what is being said. We can become further confused when someone's description of the Spirit's manifestations doesn't identify what *we* feel. With the advantage of hindsight, I can now see that my bewilderment was rooted in the misconception that a burning in the bosom was the *only* way the Spirit witnessed a message from the Lord. It never occurred to me that there were other methods in which inspiration through the Spirit was received.

The Holy Ghost plays a major role in the listening process. He is the medium through which we receive personal revelation. Therefore we need to gain a knowledge of the principles which govern his actions and to develop an awareness of his presence. To be more specific, we need to become experienced in recognizing the different methods he uses to manifest himself and in recognizing how we feel when these revelations come. Many of these methods are described in the scriptures. Let's examine a few verses to gain some insight into what others have seen, felt, and heard while listening to the Lord. These are positive, "yes" responses.

BURNING IN THE BOSOM

"But, behold, I say unto you, that you must study it out in your mind; then you must ask me if it be right, and if it is right I will cause that your bosom shall burn within you; therefore, you shall feel that it is right." (D&C 9:8.)

This is the scripture which describes a witness of the Holy Ghost as a *burning in the bosom.* It is a valid sign that the Holy Ghost has made itself manifest.

CONFIRMATION

This scripture also suggests another type of manifestation of the Spirit, that of *confirmation.* Confirmation occurs after we have spent time in the homework process and the Lord desires to confirm our plans or ideas. A girl friend of mine was seeking the Lord's approval of the man she was considering marrying. She thought for a number of days about the young man—his character traits, personality, and commitment to the Church. She considered how he honored his priesthood and how he treated her. As she evaluated these points she felt good about their relationship, so she decided to fast and pray to know the Lord's will.

In her prayer she expressed to the Lord all she liked about the young man and then asked if this young man was right for her. Suddenly she felt an urge to stop and to take an accounting of what she was feeling. She relates: "I was filled with a spirit of thankfulness, and I knew this was right. I told the Lord I didn't need to be asking for a new revelation. He had already told me." This young lady realized that the Lord was endorsing the things she had pondered and studied out. Her emotions of gratitude were a confirmation from the Spirit that she had received an answer.

The point is that confirmation can come in various ways and with different impressions. While this is an illustration of a confirmation revealed through thankfulness, sometimes the confirmation may be expressed through comfort, peace, joy, or enthusiasm.

PEACE OF MIND

"Verily, verily, I say unto you, if you desire a further witness, cast your mind upon the night that you cried unto me in your heart, that you might know concerning the truth of these things. Did I not speak peace to your mind concerning the matter? What greater witness can you have than from God?" (D&C 6:22-23.) This scripture portrays a witness of the Holy Ghost as a *peace of mind*. Note that these verses, like the one from section 9 quoted earlier, were directed to Oliver Cowdery. Different from the Lord's description of revelation to him in section nine, here the Lord reminds Oliver of a peace of mind which he had received as a witness of the Spirit.

INSTRUCTION

"Verily, verily, I say unto thee, blessed art thou for what thou hast done; for thou hast inquired of me, and behold, as often as thou hast inquired thou hast received instruction of my Spirit." (D&C 6:14.)

Here the Lord explains that he gives *instructions* through the Spirit. Instructions may come in response to a request for directions to follow or counsel to solve a problem. While working at the Missionary Training Center I taught an Elder who had learned to read only two years prior to his mission because he had dyslexia (a learning disability wherein one sees letters and words backwards). He was very dedicated to his calling as a missionary, yet memorizing the discussions was a difficult task. As his teacher I sought the Lord for counsel to make it easier for the Elder to learn the discussions. The Lord instructed me to draw pictures which depicted the content of the concepts and have him memorize by explaining the sketches. The next day I went to work on the Lord's plan. Although the Elder still struggled, this method made memorizing the discussions 100 percent easier. As I knelt in prayer that evening my heart overflowed with gratitude to the Lord for the love he showed this Elder by giving me the instructions to help him fill his calling.

ENLIGHTENING

"Behold, thou knowest that thou hast inquired of me and I did enlighten thy mind; and now I tell thee these things that thou mayest know that thou hast been enlightened by the Spirit of truth." (D&C 6:15.) An *enlightening of the mind* is another form of revelation. President Spencer W. Kimball said, "Sometimes ideas flood our minds as we listen after our prayers." ("Pray Always," p. 5.) My experience with what I term "being enlightened" could be described as a brainstorm that clarifies a confusing situation or presents a new way to see an old concept.

One morning I gazed out of my window and noticed the snow-stricken earth giving way to the dawn of spring. Observing the new birth in nature's weatherbeaten countenance aroused such excitement inside me that I was moved to my knees in grateful prayer. Though I longed to express myself, no words seemed to describe the exhilaration of my soul, so I pondered and allowed my swollen heart to render my emotions to God. Contemplating the delicacy of a budding flower and the strength of the towering trees led me to a curious question: If this telestial world is so exquisite and inspiring, what could God have created to make a terrestrial sphere more glorious? As I pursued this thought, the answer suddenly came: "The difference between a telestial and a terrestrial sphere is not in the beauties of grass, shrubs, animal life, or terrain, rather it is that a terrestrial sphere has no thorns, thistles, and weeds. Furthermore, a terrestrial sphere produces flowers and fruits spontaneously, while the opposite is true of a telestial sphere. As these thoughts filled my mind I truly felt I had been enlightened by the Spirit. (Just as a sidelight, when the question arose as to how a celestial sphere differs from a telestial or terrestrial sphere, I felt impressed that I had not studied enough to be enlightened with that knowledge.)

TO MIND AND HEART

"Yea, behold, I will tell you in your mind and in your heart, by the Holy Ghost, which shall come upon you and which shall dwell in your heart. Now, behold, this is the spirit of revelation." (D&C 8:2-3.) According to this scripture, revelation from the Lord comes to our *minds and hearts.* This too suggests various methods involved in receiving revelation. Usually instructions and ideas come to the mind, while feelings and emotions are impressed upon the heart.

COMFORT

"And I will pray the Father, and he shall give you another Comforter, that he may abide with you for ever; even the Spirit of truth; whom the world cannot receive, because it seeth him not, neither knoweth him: but ye know him for he dwelleth with you, and shall be in you. I will not leave you comfortless: I will come to you." (John 14:16-18.) Here Christ refers to the Holy Ghost as *the Comforter.* This is a descriptive name. He is called this because many times the presence of the Spirit is recognized by a comforting feeling. Comfort is usually bestowed in times of distress and sorrow.

STILL SMALL VOICE

"Yea, thus saith the still small voice, which whispereth through and pierceth all things, and often times it maketh my bones to quake while it maketh manifest. . . . (D&C 85:6.)

This is an extract from a letter of the Prophet Joseph Smith to W. W. Phelps. Notice the characteristics the Prophet used to describe the voice: still, small, whispereth, pierceth, bones to quake. The word *whisper* carries an interesting connotation. Perhaps the Lord uses *whisper* to emphasize the need to listen. Does it not require more effort on the part of the listener to hear a whisper?

JOY

"Verily, verily I say unto you, I will impart unto you of my Spirit, which shall enlighten your mind, which shall fill your soul with joy." (D&C 11:13.)

"After they had spoken these words the Spirit of the Lord came upon them, and they were filled with joy, having received a remission of their sins, and having peace of conscience because of the exceeding faith which they had in Jesus Christ who should come." (Mosiah 4:3.)

The first of the above two scriptures is the Lord's description to Hyrum Smith of the Spirit's presence. The second scripture is an account of the reaction of the people to King Benjamin's speech. These verses characterize another type of manifestation of the Holy Spirit, that of *being filled with joy*. My emotions after experiences, such as hearing a moving talk or going to an inspiring meeting could be described as "filled with joy." To me, being filled with joy is a bursting or overwhelming sensation. Sometimes when I experience the Spirit in this way, I possess a great enthusiasm in relation to what I am praying about. The word *enthusiasm* evolved from the Greek word *enthousiasmos* which means having divine influence or being divinely inspired. It could be said that when a person is filled with the Spirit, he is filled with enthusiasm. These types of feelings usually accompany a confirmation or positive answer from the Lord.

STUPOR OF THOUGHT

Of course, sometimes the Lord may want to communicate no to our question or disapproval of our decision. He has varying methods of revealing this response. One way he does this is explained in the Doctrine and Covenants wherein the Lord says: "But if it be not right you shall have no such feeling, but you shall have a stupor of thought that shall cause you to forget the thing which is wrong." (D&C 9:9.) Sometimes an actual forgetting of the thought occurs. It has been my experience, however, that I have not forgotten the idea or question, but rather I have forgotten my desire or enthusiasm to do or say those things I was inquiring about. Once I was trying to make a decision as to whether to go away and attend college or stay home. After some personal contemplation, I decided to go to college and was excited about leaving. I took my decision to the Lord to ask his approval. From that moment and through the next couple of days my desire and enthusiasm to go to school seemed to die until finally I did not wish to go. Although I could still remember my decision about entering college, I had lost or forgotten my desire to go.

A CONTRASTING FEELING

This scripture also gives us another insight on what to expect when the Lord does not agree with our decision or idea. "But if it be not right you shall have no such feeling" [a burning in the bosom, a positive feeling], "but you shall have a stupor of thought" [a contrasting feeling]. Here the Lord teaches that he reveals that something is not right with a feeling which is in contrast to a positive answer. In this case a stupor of thought. From this we see that the Lord communicates disapproval with impressions that are opposite to the types of feelings or revelations we receive when a request is approved.

Let's compare some scriptures which describe contrasting feelings. In Mosiah 26:13 we read: "And now the spirit of Alma was again troubled; and he went and inquired of the Lord what he should do concerning this matter." Being troubled might be contrasted to feeling peace of mind or feeling comforted. Doctrine and Covenants 10:2 states: "And you also lost your gift at the same time, and your mind became darkened." Having a darkened mind is opposite to being enlightened or receiving instructions. These are some of the ways the Lord communicates no or disapproval to us.

DEVELOPING THE SKILL OF LISTENING

Since there are various methods in which the Spirit manifests itself, learning to recognize which one is being felt on any given occasion can be a challenging task. Before I realized that a witness from the Holy Ghost could come in a manner other than a burning in the bosom, I felt some real frustrations as I searched for answers to prayer. I recall that during my senior year of high school I completed reading the Book of Mormon for the first time. Although I had faith that the book contained the word of God, still I yearned to test Moroni's challenge and to receive the promised manifestation of its truthfulness through the Holy Ghost. (See Moroni 10:4.) One evening I knelt in prayer and humbly pleaded that I might receive a witness of the truth of the book. When the anticipated manifestation didn't come, I felt letdown and rejected. I almost wished I hadn't asked. I wanted to force myself to believe I had felt something, yet my inner honesty would not allow such self-deception. I now realize that the Lord chose to reveal the witness of the truth of the book as a peaceful feeling—quite a different feeling from the one I thought would come. The dilemma is evident. Obviously I needed to expand my knowledge of the Spirit's working and to develop a sensitivity to the way I felt inside when the Spirit was speaking to me.

The nature of the art of listening to God is such that it demands that each person discover and develop this skill himself. There are many reasons for this. Our individual temperaments and experiences cause us to perceive our feelings differently. Therefore, the Spirit's impressions will affect each of us in various ways under different circumstances. Furthermore, because every person's experiences with the Spirit are unique, no one can fully explain what or how another feels when a witness is received.

ALMA'S GUIDELINES HELPFUL

Although we are each responsible for acquiring this skill, we have not been left without counsel and direction. The guidelines that Alma shares for the attainment of faith can also be adapted to prayer:

> Now, as I said concerning faith—that it was not a perfect knowledge—even so it is with my words. Ye cannot know of their surety at first, unto perfection, any more than faith is a perfect knowledge.
>
> But behold, if ye will awake and arouse your faculties, even to an experiment upon my words, and exercise a particle of faith, yea, even if ye can no more than desire to believe, let this desire work in you, even until ye believe in a manner that ye can give place for a portion of my words. (Alma 32:26-27.)

Alma points out that a surety of his words does not come at first, but only through experimenting. He also stresses that we must give place for a desire if we are to be successful.

"SUDDEN STROKES OF IDEAS"

Joseph Smith once shared his impressions of how personal revelation is received. He explained:

> A person may profit by noticing the first intimation of the spirit of revelation; for instance, when you feel pure intelligence flowing into you, it may give you sudden strokes of ideas, so that by

noticing it, you may find it fulfilled the same day or soon; (i.e.) those things that were presented unto your minds by the Spirit of God, . . . and . . . by . . . understanding it, you may grow into the principle of revelation, until you become perfect in Christ Jesus. (*History of the Church*, 3:381.)

Apparently these sudden strokes of ideas can come into the mind and then only be *recognized* (in the case of an inexperienced person) upon their later fulfillment. This suggests that after the total prayer experience is fulfilled, we stop and evaluate what has happened. Joseph Smith points out that we *grow into* the principle of revelation.

EXPERIMENTING, EVALUATING, COMPARING

By applying these principles to acquiring the skill of listening to the Spirit, it appears that we can know through experimenting and evaluating how it feels to have impressions from the Spirit. A pattern or procedure emerges on how to apply the experimenting techniques. It involves learning to evaluate past interactions with the Spirit and then applying that knowledge to future encounters. Here is a suggested approach. Begin by making *proper spiritual preparation* prior to asking for anything in prayer. Then, as *prompted by the Spirit, present the matter in question to the Father. Listen to your feelings and thoughts* as you consult with God and then *draw* from them *a decision.* Keeping in mind the manner in which these feelings and thoughts came, *follow through* on the answer you perceived. Later, with the advantage of hindsight, *evaluate* what transpired as a result of your prayer.

Evaluation is a crucial part of the experiment. During this time you ponder about the answer you received to prayer. If you conclude that you were led by divine inspiration to the answer, then you know that the feeling and thoughts you had during prayer were of God. Now you are aware of one way in which you are impressed by the Spirit. Remember these feelings. In the future when this impression is given, you can be assured it is of God, and you can follow it with confidence. By continuing to experiment, you will gain a "repertoire" of types of impressions you feel from the Holy Ghost. Your inner trust in your ability to hear and understand these feelings will be strengthened. Then, as stated by Joseph Smith, "you may grow into the principle of revelation."

The prophet Alma gives some insights on how to evaluate the results of experimenting. First, he describes how to recognize what we have labeled a positive response. "If it be a true seed, or a good seed, if ye do not cast it out by your unbelief, . . . it will begin to swell within your breasts; and when you feel these swelling motions, ye will begin to say within yourselves—It must needs be that this is a good seed, . . . for it beginneth to enlarge my soul; yea, it beginneth to enlighten my understanding, yea, it beginneth to be delicious to me." (Alma 32:29.)

Next, he explains how to identify a negative (contrasting) answer. "If a seed groweth it is good, but if it groweth not, behold it is not good." (Alma 32:32.) Then he teaches us how to use the results of our answers, together with hindsight, to evaluate what we felt. "Ye have tried the experiment, and planted the seed, and it swelleth and sprouteth, and beginneth to grow, ye must needs know that the seed is good. And now, behold, is your knowledge perfect? Yea, your knowledge is perfect in that thing, . . . and this because you know, for ye know that the word hath swelled your souls, and ye also know that it hath sprouted up, that your understanding doth begin to be enlightened, and your mind doth begin to expand." (Alma 32:33-34.)

Alma concludes by expressing the rewards of persisting. "If ye will nourish the word, yea, nourish the tree as it beginneth to grow, by your faith with great diligence, and with patience, looking forward to the fruit thereof, it shall take root; and behold it shall be a tree springing up unto everlasting life." (Alma 32:41.)

I had a simple experience which illustrates the satisfaction and security that acquiring the skill of listening can bring. When I became pregnant with our first child, my husband and I began to consider moving from our studio apartment to a one-bedroom apartment. We were somewhat reluctant because the rent was one-third higher than the place in which we were living. After weighing the pros and cons of moving, we each went to the Lord in prayer. As I explained to the Lord the pros for moving, I had a disturbing feeling; but as soon as I began to present the pros for staying, a peace filled my being. Because I had felt that Spirit of peace before, I knew immediately that we were to stay in our present home. It felt good to be able to return to my husband and to report with confidence my response from the Lord. Likewise he came to me with the same answer. The reason why I understood the Spirit's witness is that I had applied the knowledge I had gained through previous interactions with the Spirit.

This same technique of comparing past encounters with the Spirit to identify present feelings can be adapted to other situations. After an uplifting meeting, while reading scriptures, or during an inspiring conversation you may recognize the Spirit's presence. On occasion someone may announce that the Spirit has been manifest in great abundance, thus disclosing to you the source of your immediate emotions. By applying the experimenting techniques to these types of experiences you can identify more of the types of impressions the Spirit gives you and thus aid the further development of your listening skills.

Analyzing these techniques clears up some of the misinformation about how revelation is received. First, it falsifies the notion that from the initial moment the Spirit speaks to you, you will recognize those promptings ever afterwards and know they are from God. It also does away with the misconceptions that imply that revelation always comes like a "thunderbolt." Don't be surprised if the Spirit's presence isn't as spectacular as you had expected or if its witness isn't as obvious as you had anticipated. (See I Kings 19:11-13.) From small beginnings we grow in our ability to receive and perceive revelation.

Experimenting with the skill of listening to the Lord is an involved process and it requires relentless dedication. Initially it can be a perplexing and sometimes a discouraging process.

MASTERING THE ART

I've found that personal revelation comes to me in varying ways, depending on my questions and the circumstances. When I am seeking counsel or answers, the Spirit's messages are sometimes manifest as fleeting ideas that leave as quickly as they come. Recognizing and snatching onto them has been a challenging process. At first I was bewildered because these ideas appeared to originate in my own mind and didn't seem divinely inspired. But my bewilderment disappeared as I came to better understand the workings of the Spirit. After receiving the gift of the Holy Ghost, we sometimes become so accustomed to his influence that when he impresses us with an idea we ignorantly assume it was self-originated and not divinely inspired. Now I realize that if I have prepared properly for prayer, these thoughts are not mine but the Lord's. Thus, I have tried to become sensitive to these fleeting moments of inspiration and to acknowledge them as coming from God.

Another way I have come to recognize an inner manifestation of the Spirit is as an exhilarating or excited feeling. This feeling usually comes as the result of attending an inspiring meeting, setting goals, or learning a new concept. It also accompanies a positive or go-ahead-as-planned response from the Lord.

In times of trial or distress I realize the Spirit's presence as a comforting feeling. Usually I am blessed with comfort when I am saddened or upset.

Other times the Spirit brings a peace. This is especially true when my problems are staring me in the face and I can't see the light at the end of the tunnel. When these situations arise, the peace is sometimes accompanied by strength which allows me to continue bearing up; the peace may bring an easing of the burden, indicating an approach of relief or an expelling of the difficulty.

Acquiring the skill of recognizing, understanding, and working with personal revelation is a challenge worthy of our mightiest efforts. It is common to find the road to success as an unused footpath in a fog that dissipates only enough to expose the next step. Our Heavenly Father bids us to come unto him, to know him, to be with him. Through his prophets he has given us the keys to mastering the skill of seeing clearly in the clouds of confusion. Recalling again Alma's counsel, "Because ye have tried the experiment, and planted the seed, and it swelleth and sprouteth, and beginneth to grow, ye must needs know that the seed is good," we can associate with it Joseph Smith's statement: "The things of God are of deep import; and time, and experience, and careful and ponderous and solemn thoughts can only find them out." (*History of the Church*, 3:295.)

As we persist in experimenting, evaluating, and applying learned knowledge, we will master the art of listening to God's communications to us. The crowning highlight will be the deepening of our relationship with our Heavenly Father.

Making a Commitment *Chapter 9*

R eceiving personal revelation from the Lord brings with it the responsibility of commitment. When we make a commitment, we promise the Lord that we will accept his counsel and pursue our lives in accordance with it.

CONSISTENCY OF COMMITMENT NECESSARY

Demonstrating a consistency in committing ourselves to do all the things revealed during prayer will insure the Lord's willingness to continue to answer our future pleas. If we choose not to follow through with the Lord's counsel, we forfeit our right to more revelation.

This principle is alluded to in a story President Spencer W. Kimball related while speaking at a Brigham Young University devotional in September 1979. He said that President Brigham Young spoke at a stake conference in a town in southern Utah and admonished the people to clean up their yards and fix their old barns. A year later he returned to speak in the same stake. As he traveled into town he noticed that the yards were still cluttered and the barns were still not repaired. When he stood to give his talk he told the people he wasn't going to tell them anything new because they had not done what he had asked them to do previously. Because of their neglecting to follow his first admonition, he felt it would be useless to give the people further counsel. They had not committed themselves to follow the prophet's word.

Perhaps a hypothetical situation can emphasize the importance of commitment as a part of prayer. Let's suppose that a friend comes to you with a problem and asks for your counsel. As you listen you begin to empathize with him. You feel good that he thought of you as a person he could turn to when he was in need. Lovingly you share your most sincere advice. Later you learn that he didn't consider your suggestions good enough even to try them. Now he is still complaining and struggling over the same issue. If he returned with another problem, would you feel the same urgency to help? If he repeatedly ignored your guidance, would that not affect your desire to offer your suggestions again?

The Lord's desire to give us further revelation is dampened when we disregard his counsel, thus rejecting, incidentally, the guaranteed best advice for the situation. Christ informs us of the ultimate outcome of such neglect:

"For whosoever *receiveth,* to him shall be given, and he shall have more abundance; but whosoever *continueth not to receive,* from him shall be taken away even that he hath." (Matthew 13:10-11, Joseph Smith Translation; emphasis added. See also Alma 12:9-11.)

MAKING COMMITMENTS EFFECTIVELY

Since committing ourselves to do God's will has such a significant influence on our receiving answers to prayer, it is essential that we acquire the ability to make commitments effectively. The scriptures again provide a source of instruction.

First it is important that we be *specific* in the things we commit ourselves to do. After descending from the mountain with the Ten Commandments, Moses explained in detail to the children of Israel what was expected of them before they made the covenant to be obedient. "And Moses came and told the people all the words of the Lord . . . and all the people answered with one voice, and said, All the words which the Lord hath said will we do." (Exodus 24:3.) As we make a covenant with God, we need to itemize clearly what we are going to do. When appropriate, we should also set a time specification.

Second, we should *write* down our commitments. Exodus 24:4 explains that after the children of Israel had made the covenant to be obedient, "Moses wrote all the words of the Lord." Writing the particulars of our commitment will firm them up in our minds.

Third, we must be *determined* to fulfill our commitments. In Doctrine and Covenants 20:37 the Lord explains what is required of a person who wants to enter into the covenant of baptism: "a determination to serve him to the end." We need this same determination in fulfilling all our commitments. In fact, without determination our commitments are just words.

Determination is a developed character trait. It begins as a decision made within and continues as a drive that motivates us toward success. Determination is a belief in ourselves that is strengthened as we use it and an ability that increases through repeated success. Mastering the ability to determine our course will tremendously aid us in honoring our commitments.

COMMITMENT BRINGS STEWARDSHIP

The act of making a commitment to the Lord brings upon us a stewardship. This stewardship entails remembering the terms of the agreement, following through with the commitments, and reporting back to the Lord. Let's discuss each of these.

We should not expect the Lord to manifest his will to us on a given matter more than once, especially when clearly we have understood that will. It is our obligation to remember the revelation and our commitment to follow it.

I had an experience which illustrates our responsibility to *remember* the witnesses and covenants we make with the Lord. Shortly before our marriage my husband and I had a discussion on when to begin our family. I wanted to wait a year so I could finish college, but my husband felt we should follow the prophet's counsel not to put off starting a family. Together we went to the Lord in prayer. But because I had already made up my mind to some extent about what I wanted to do, the impressions that were given to my husband were not clear in my mind. Thus, my husband felt we should not wait to begin our family while I believed we should. Patiently he then decided it would be best if we were united on the subject before having children, and he conceded to waiting. Unbeknown to me, he continued to pray that I would receive a testimony of the counsel the Lord had revealed to him.

A few months later we were invited to a friend's wedding in the Manti Temple. As the ceremony progressed, there came into my mind the thought that the commandment to bear children was from the Lord and was not a personal opinion of my husband or of the prophet which we could adjust to our own circumstances.

The next day was fast Sunday, so I decided to make this subject the object of my fast. Kneeling in prayer to begin my fast, I explained the events of the past day and asked for a confirmation of this counsel. At the time my husband and I were team teaching the gospel doctrine class in a Brigham Young University ward. As I was presenting my portion of the lesson, somehow this very subject came up. Although I had not mentioned my situation, two or three of the class members bore testimony of the happiness they had received by not delaying the start of their families. They further testified of the growth they had received as they saw the Lord provide the financial means for meeting this challenge. In fast and testimony meeting that day the same types of testimonies were borne. Later as I pondered and prayed before breaking my fast, I had a warm feeling inside confirming that the Lord had verified his will to me, and I made a commitment to follow it.

My challenge came as the days passed and time began to dim the impressions of the Spirit. I was left to myself to remember the testimony I had received and the covenant I had made with the Lord. As I again became engrossed in school I found myself questioning the witness I had received and returning to my former desires of finishing college first. I considered approaching the Lord for another manifestation, in hopes that I may have reached the wrong conclusion about what had happened. Then I reached back to the thoughts and feelings of the fast day experience, and I knew I must assume my responsibility to remember the Lord's revelation and my covenant to follow it.

Another part of commitment stewardship concerns our responsibility to *follow through.* It is important to realize the extent of the binding power in a covenant to the Lord. Covenants are sacred and are not to be taken lightly or made without the deepest intent to follow through. When we make a contract with the Lord to do his will, he expects us to exert all our energies to do as we have promised. A breach of contract is a personal offense to God and a serious violation of his trust in our word, as we see by Doctrine and Covenants section 104. Soon after the organization of the Church, the Lord desired to establish the United Order among his people. As the members were called upon to live this principle, they were required to enter into a covenant with the Lord. When it became evident to the Lord that the covenant had been broken, he warned: "For I, the Lord, am not to be mocked in these things. . . . Therefore, inasmuch as you are found transgressors, you cannot escape my wrath in your lives." (D&C 104:6, 8.)

As we make covenants to follow the Lord's will, we must also be aware that the Lord may allow us to pass through trials to prove the depth of our commitment to do as we have promised. He cautioned the earlier Saints: "I have decreed in my heart, saith the Lord, that I will prove you in all things, whether you will abide in my covenant, even unto death, that you may be found worthy." (D&C 98:14.) Thus, when we make a covenant with the Lord we must be determined to follow through.

To complete our stewardship, it is appropriate through prayer to *report our progress to the Lord.* This will also help us to strengthen our commitment and to impress the covenant upon our memories.

In this connection I recall an experience from my single days. After having made a covenant with the Lord in prayer not to see any R-rated movies, I was invited on a date by a young man I was becoming attracted to. When he asked if I would like to see a certain movie with him, I responded with an energetic yes. After I hung up the phone, I realized that I did not know the rating of the show. At first I wanted to ignore the thought, rationalizing that ignorance wasn't a sin. Then I realized that by that acknowledgment alone, I was not ignorant.

Reluctantly I scanned the newspaper to find the rating. It was an R-rated film. At first I was devastated, because I really wanted to go out with the young man. But as I contemplated having to report this incident to the Lord, I received the necessary strength to do what I knew I had to. Although the young man never asked me out again after I broke the date, that disappointment was minor compared with the joy I received when I reported my actions to the Lord. I didn't have to repent of any wrongdoing but I had only to thank him for the strength he had blessed me with to do what was right.

As we accept the stewardship of remembering, following through, and reporting that accompanies commitment, we will be successful. But there are reasons and circumstances that keep us from making covenants. Let's analyze a few and hope that by recognizing them we can overcome them.

FEAR OF FAILURE

The serious nature of a covenant sometimes creates a fear that we may fail. This fear of betraying our word can cause us to be leery of making a commitment to the Lord. Ideally we should be completely confident in our ability to keep commitments, yet it is not uncommon to feel some inner anxiety. We should not let these anxieties intimidate us to the extent of interfering with our power to make commitments.

The effects fear can have on our ability to make a commitment can be seen in the parable of the talents. The Lord gave talents to three servants, apparently with the understanding that they were to improve upon them. The first two servants accepted the Lord's challenge and committed to themselves to do as he had commanded. However, the third servant did not accept his stewardship to honor the commitment the Lord had offered him. His excuse was, "I was afraid, and went and hid thy talent in the earth." (Matthew 25:25.)

Fear of making commitments keeps us from receiving the Lord's blessings. "Ye endeavored to believe that ye should receive the blessing which was offered unto you; . . . but . . . there were fears in your hearts, and verily this is the reason that ye did not receive." (D&C 67:3.)

INADEQUATE DESIRE

Another reason why we refrain from making covenants is that we do not possess sufficient desire or determination to do completely what the Lord has counseled. This happened to me when the Church's edition of the Bible and the new edition of the other three scriptures were published. My husband latched onto a copy of each and began using them immediately. He kept telling me how exciting it was to use them in study and teaching. Of course, I was attached to my old standby set which I had taken on my mission and had marked and cross-referenced. Still, I was aware of the prophet's counsel to use the new editions.

One week in Sunday School the lesson was solely on the need to use the new editions of the scriptures. As the teacher read from Elder Boyd K. Packer's October 1982 general conference talk and testified of the aid the new editions had been in her life, I felt somewhat moved that I should reconsider. But I just couldn't give up my old versions. So I told the Lord I would obtain a copy of the new editions and carry them around with my old set. I decided the least I could do was read out of the new ones; and when I needed to look up a scripture, I could use my old ones. Since I couldn't relinquish my old editions completely, I felt this would be a good start. I was open-minded enough to desire that I might begin to enjoy using the new editions.

The Lord did bless me with a desire to use the new editions. Needless to say, after exploring the new set for only a short while I was amazed at my former reluctance. The new editions have made scripture study even more exciting than before.

My experience illustrates a principle and a solution. The principle is that it is to our advantage to commit ourselves to follow the Lord's will completely. But, when circumstances or lack of determination inhibit our ability or desire to make a total commitment, there is an alternative available. Because I was not fully committed myself to do as the Lord had commanded, I did not make a total commitment. Instead I promised to do as much as I believed I could honestly live up to. When we use this alternative it is important to request help from God that in the near future we can increase our commitment to meet the entire challenge. The point should be made that if the alternate course is chosen, the blessings will be received or forfeited in proportion to our degree of commitment.

We should also be warned that our demonstrating a slowness or reluctance to follow the Lord's counsel may result in a slower response from him in the next request. This is evidenced in the early history of the Church in Missouri. The people had been slow to follow the Lord's instructions; so when they sought the Lord's help in a time of affliction, he replied:

They were slow to hearken unto the voice of the Lord their God; therefore, the Lord their God is slow to hearken unto their prayers, to answer them in the day of their trouble.

In the day of their peace they esteemed lightly my counsel; but in the day of their trouble, of necessity they feel after me. (D&C 101:7-8.)

PERSONAL BENEFITS FROM COMMITMENT

Committing ourselves to the Lord in prayer to follow his word offers many benefits and blessings. First, it allows us the opportunity to acknowledge and affirm *to ourselves* the impressions we received in response to our prayers. Second, it grants an occasion to the Lord to confirm that we have interpreted his message correctly, thereby intensifying the initial witness received from the Spirit. Third, and most important, the act of making a commitment to the Lord to carry out his will strengthens our desire to accomplish what he has counseled us to do and binds us to be accountable to him for our actions.

As we commit ourselves to do what the Lord has asked, we allow him the opportunity to bless us for following his counsel. The Lord affirms this in Doctrine and Covenants 82:10: "I, the Lord, am bound when ye do what I say; but when ye do not what I say, ye have no promise."

COVENANTING FOR SPECIAL BLESSINGS

There is a unique type of commitment that is appropriate to discuss here—that of covenanting to receive special blessings. When so impressed by the Spirit, we can promise to do something in return for a needed blessing. While serving a mission, my companion and I would covenant with the Lord that we would put in extra hours of work for a blessing from him to lead us to someone who was searching for the truth. A similar kind of experience occurred to a friend of mine. He was studying for a test when asked to perform an act of service. He covenanted with the Lord to render the service if God would help him prepare for the test in a shorter length of time. He later commented: "The information just came together, and I did well on my test."

I stress here that covenanting for a blessing is not a type of bargaining table wherein we decide what we want and negotiate terms. There are principles we must adhere to. First, the act should be in balance with the blessing requested. Second and most important, the covenanting in exchange for a blessing requires a confirmation from the Spirit that what we are asking is in accordance with God's will.

COVENANTS—HONORED AND DISHONORED

Speaking of some earlier Church members, the Lord made clear his thoughts and feelings concerning those who honored and those who dishonored a certain covenant with him: "And as the covenant which they made unto me has been broken, even so it has become void and of none effect. And wo to him by whom this offense cometh, for it had been better for him that he had been drowned in the depth of the sea." On the other hand, "Blessed are they who have kept the covenant and observed the commandment, for they shall obtain mercy" (D&C 54:4-6.) And in another connection: "Verily I say unto you, all among them who know their hearts are honest, and are broken, and their spirits contrite, and are willing to observe their covenants by sacrifice—yea every sacrifice which I, the Lord, shall command—they are accepted of me. (D&C 97:8.) Such scriptures suggest the importance of honoring our covenants with the Lord.

Making and honoring covenants is an eternal principle which we must become proficient in if we are to progress through eternity and become as God is. Again, prayer provides the laboratory in which we can perfect this ability.

Closing the Prayer Chapter 10

The Savior explained that we should always offer our prayers in his name, promising that if we do so in righteousness they will be heard and answered. "Therefore ye must always pray unto the Father in my name; And whatsoever ye shall ask the Father in my name, which is right, believing that ye shall receive, behold it shall be given unto you." (3 Nephi 18:19-20.)

IN THE NAME OF JESUS CHRIST

Praying in this manner suggests to me the role Christ plays in our relationship with the Father. In a sense we might look upon prayer as a symbol of the Atonement, because we can let it remind us that Christ is the Mediator between God and man. The dictionary defines *mediator* as a person who settles differences between two parties. One of its synonyms is reconciler. When Christ is described as the Mediator between God and man, it means that through his atoning sacrifice he offers sinful man the means to be cleansed and thereby be reconciled with sinless God. He earned this title when he suffered for the sins of mankind in the Garden of Gethsemane, giving us the opportunity to repent and receive forgiveness. When he died and was resurrected, he opened the door of resurrection to all of God's children.

An interesting aspect of the closing phrase of prayer is the use of the word *amen*. In Hebrew *amen* means truly, faithfully, and it denotes acceptance. In English it means so be it. Elder Bruce R. McConkie explains that amen is also one of Christ's names (see Revelation 3:14), that it is "a title given to show that it is in and through him that the seal of divine affirmation is placed on all the promises of the Father." (*Mormon Doctrine*, p. 32.)

Daily prayer closed in Jesus Christ's name can be a continual reminder of him, his atonement, and the gifts and opportunities God gives to us.

Remaining
on the Knees

Chapter 11

A lthough we utter the word *amen* signaling the formal close
of the prayer, we need to continually remember our relationship with our Father and commune with him throughout the
day. Remaining on our knees after prayer provides an invaluable
preparation period in which we can ponder what has happened,
make plans to follow the counsel we have received, and resolve
to fulfill the commitments we have made. Most importantly, in
this time we can make provision to take the Spirit with us.

MOMENTS AFTER PRAYER

The moments following prayer are quality time that can be
reserved for pondering and setting goals to achieve and for
honoring the commitments just made. Inasmuch as the Spirit is
still present in good measure, it is a time of good sensitivity to
the Lord's promptings. He will continue to influence our
thoughts while we are pondering, and he will direct us to set
solid goals that will lead us to succeed.

A young man related to me this experience which illustrates
the continued inspiration that comes immediately after prayer.
Once while steadily dating a girl he began to lose control of his

76

thoughts. When he realized this, he knew he must repent and bridle his passions or they would begin to manipulate the situation. He went to the Lord in prayer and repented. He made a commitment to restrain his emotions and control his thoughts. He further pleaded for help that he would have the motivation to be successful. At the close of his prayer he recognized that although he felt strongly about his commitment, there was still the risk of losing sight of this promise in some situations when with his girl friend. As he pondered after his prayer, a story Elder Robert L. Simpson had related came to his mind.

In his recollection of the story, Elder Simpson had told of a fighter pilot who had made a special oath to himself in connection with his job. The air force required that its pilots navigate their planes at least two hundred feet above the tree line, but this pilot decided that that level was not safe enough for him. He made a commitment to himself to stay at least five hundred feet above the trees. In this he would make sure he would never be tempted to break the air force regulation.

As the young man thought about this story, he decided that he too must make a "five-hundred-foot" commitment to keep himself from being tempted to break his covenant with the Lord. He promised himself to always have his date home by midnight, to avoid being in a secluded place with her alone, and to immediately reject unholy thoughts. He testified that these personal covenants were exactly what he needed to do to feel secure about his ability to honor his covenant with the Lord. These thoughts all came to him while pondering after praying. I consider his experience a good example of how the Lord will give us additional light if after prayer we will take time to remain on our knees for pondering and setting goals to fill our commitments.

We can also use this time to write down the thoughts, feelings, and commitments that resulted from prayer. This is what the Lord commanded Joseph Smith and Signey Rigdon to do at the close of the vision of the three degrees of glory recorded in Doctrine and Covenants 76. Verse 113 states: "This is the end of the vision which we saw, which we were commanded to write while we were yet in the Spirit." There are many reasons for the Lord's counsel to write while in the Spirit. First, making a record of your revelations and covenants will help you remember them and strengthen your commitment to do them. A journal record can be of great assistance in this endeavor. A journal is also an excellent place in which to record the goals you set to carry out your commitments. Having a record of your goals is beneficial because you can review them periodically to refresh your memory and to strengthen your desire to fill them. It can also be a great comfort and strength to you in times of depression as well as in times of joy.

These journal entries can be of aid to you in the experimenting process discussed in Chapter 8. Feelings and impressions that are recorded while in the spirit of prayer will help you identify what you are feeling and clarify what is being said. When writing with the Spirit, your words tend to more accurately describe what you are feeling and thinking. What an exciting and testimony-building experience it will be to read how and when a revelation was received! Then a few entries later read of its fulfillment.

The desire to write does not have to be suppressed until after prayer. Sometimes it is beneficial to take time to write while in the midst of receiving revelation. This is especially helpful when you have a number of things to approach the Lord about. By recording each revelation when receiving it, you can give your full attention to the next subject.

Even if we have nothing to record, the time following prayer can be beneficial. Possibly the greatest benefit is that this time can be used as a transition period. In this period we leave the intimacy of God's presence and make provision to take the Spirit with us as we enter man's world. When genuine communication has taken place during prayer, we feel a natural desire to remain on our knees and to bask in the Spirit which has been present.

We have no disposition to jump up, run out of God's presence, and turn on the radio or TV.

As we strive to retain the spirit and attitude of prayer throughout the day, we will be receptive to additional inspiration. One afternoon my husband called me from work to say hello. When I inquired how his day was going, he replied, "Lousy," and shared a few evidences to support his evaluation. As I got off the phone and resumed my housework I received an impression to stop work and to pray that things would improve for my husband that day. I did, and then the incident left my mind. When he returned that evening, I routinely inquired how his day had been. He said that after he had talked to me things improved and the day turned out pretty well. It was then that I remembered my impression to pray. I felt grateful that I was in tune so I could recognize and follow the Spirit's promptings.

ANSWERS MAY COME LATER

There are times when the answers to our prayers do not come when we are on our knees. Often this occurs when the nature of the request is such that its fulfillment is to take place later, or perhaps the Lord is waiting to reveal a solution but first we need to initiate some action to bring about his aid.

While serving as spiritual living teacher in Relief Society, circumstances arose which required me to be out of town on the Sunday of my lesson a week or two later. In anticipation of finding a substitute I considered several sisters who I thought would be well qualified to teach the lesson. Sunday morning before I left for church I knelt in prayer to ask the Lord to help me find someone to teach the lesson. I received a confident feeling that he would lead me to the right person. I took my books to church and approached a number of sisters, but none of them was available to teach. With my books still in hand I returned home.

79

As I sat down at the phone, I noticed the ward list was open, and the name of a sister caught my eye. Then the impression to call her came, and I dialed the number. After I had made the request, she inquired which lesson I wanted her to take, and asked if she could call me back in an hour. In her return call she said she would be glad to teach the lesson and shared the following experience.

Earlier in the year she had gone through some depressing times. One day during that period she took out the Relief Society manual and flipped to this very lesson. As she read the lesson she had a moving interaction with the Spirit. This caused her to make some decisions and commitments to improve. From then on things had been getting progressively better. When I asked her to teach the lesson, her initial reaction was to say no. Because she was a recent convert, she felt inadequate to teach a spiritual living lesson to the sisters. But after reading the lesson again and recalling her experience, the Spirit moved her to take the challenge.

I went out of town as planned, and a few days after the lesson had been given, while I was speaking with the Relief Society president, I asked how the lesson had gone. She replied that I couldn't have found a better person for the task. The teacher had presented the lesson in a way no other person could have, and the sisters had been really touched. It was clear to me that no one but the Lord could have known of this sister's spiritual experience and her consequent ability to handle the lesson in such a personal and moving manner.

Many times when the request is to be fulfilled later, some type of witness is given during the prayer to assure us that the Lord has heard our plea. It was so in this case—a comforting feeling that things would work out. The actual inspiration as to who was to teach the lesson and her acceptance didn't come until later.

These types of experiences will come to us as we invest the time and gain the skill necessary to have meaningful communication with God each day. Prayer should invite and intensify the presence of the Spirit.

PURPOSES OF REMAINING ON KNEES

The objectives of remaining on our knees are:

1. To furnish a period in which we can ponder and evaluate our thoughts and feelings about what we said and experienced during the prayer.

2. To allow time for planning and setting goals to carry out the commitments made.

3. To allow a moment "while in the Spirit" to make a record of the proceedings of our prayer, covenants, and emotions.

4. Most importantly, to provide a period in which we can prepare to invite the Spirit, which we have felt intensely through communication with God, to guide us during the day.

These moments of solitude acknowledge the wonder and the privilege of being able to converse with God. They make our prayers more meaningful and our lives more fulfilled.

Our Challenge

O ur Heavenly Father has commanded us to approach him often in prayer, since prayer is directly linked to the attainment of his goal for us—to bring "to pass the immortality and eternal life of man." (Moses 1:39.) Our Father desires that we choose to accept his goal as our own. Thus he has revealed what we must do to attain eternal life with him—basically, keep all his commandments. As to what constitutes eternal life, God has declared through his Son, "This is life eternal, that they might know thee the only true God, and Jesus Christ, whom thou hast sent." (John 17:3.)

COMING TO KNOW GOD

Somewhere, then, we have to come to know God. In reference to our pre-earth life, Brigham Young commented that each of us is "well acquainted with God our Heavenly Father. . . . for there is not a soul of you but what has lived with him year after year." (John A. Widtsoe, comp., *Discourses of Brigham Young,* Deseret Book Co., 1954, p. 50.) But it is apparent that that experience, wherein we were untested and untried by mortality and we walked by sight rather than by faith, is insufficient to the purpose. In preparation for eternal life, to whatever extent possible we need to come to know God while on this earth.

While this is a lifetime task, the scriptures encourage us in it. John wrote:

Beloved, let us love one another: for love is of God; and every one that loveth is born of God, and knoweth God. (1 John 4:7.) Speaking of Church members who endure to the end in righteousness, the Lord said:

> For behold, in my name are they called; and if they know me they shall come forth, and shall have a place eternally at my right hand. (Mosiah 26:24.)

On the other hand:

> For strait is the gate, and narrow the way that leadeth unto the exaltation and continuation of the lives, and few there be that find it, because ye receive me not in the world neither do ye know me. (D&C 132:22.)

The concept of knowing God implies developing our relationship with him as our Heavenly Father. Essential to this development is our experiencing daily two-way communication in prayer. Elder Bruce R. McConkie said: "No accountable person ever has or ever will gain celestial rest unless he learns to communicate with the Master of that realm." ("Why the Lord Ordained Prayer," p. 9.)

Building a relationship requires that both parties invest quality time together in openly sharing and honestly listening. In developing our relationship with God, we must devote time to meaningful communication with him. Such time may be found during scripture study, temple sessions, and prayer. This communication helps to prepare for eternal life by coming to know God better and by becoming more comfortable in his presence.

ADEQUATE TIME FOR PRAYER

Some years back, in a class I attended, the teacher challenged each one present to spend twenty minutes a day in prayer for the next two weeks. My first reaction was, *You're crazy! No way can I pray for twenty minutes a day!* I promptly dismissed the idea from my mind. Later that evening while reviewing my notes of that class, however, I began to ponder that challenge. I decided to make the attempt.

The next morning found me on my knees, clock by my side, resolved to give my first twenty-minute offering to the Lord. After saying everything appropriate I could think of, I peeked at the clock. Only four minutes had passed. I still had sixteen minutes to go. So I just stayed there and waited. Twenty minutes finally passed. Apart from the carpet impressions on my knees, I didn't feel much different. I arose and went on with the day.

The procedure was about the same the next day, but during the first day I had taken a few mental notes of something to talk about, so now I spent only the last fourteen minutes in silence.

Around the fourth day, as I was biding out the remainder of my time in silence, an idea came to me. I decided I might as well talk about it as just kneel there, so I vocalized my thought. Then another thought came to me, and I expressed it to the Lord. Again the twenty minutes ended, and I concluded my prayer.

Each day I continued to receive these ideas of what to talk about. Voicing them made my twenty-minute prayer more enjoyable, so I kept on sharing them with the Lord. The unexpected surprise came as the days progressed. When a problem would arise, the "thoughts" I had expressed during prayer seemed to present a logical answer, or if I pursued an "idea," a difficulty would fall into place. As I observed these happenings, I became aware that these "thoughts and ideas" were actually impressions of the Spirit.

My prayers became more meaningful as I comprehended the fact that God was actually talking to me. By the end of the two-week challenge I felt closer to my Father than ever before. I looked forward to prayer and determined that I would set aside twenty minutes every day to spend with God. This resolution provided an avenue for me to develop the skill found in the two-way-communication process of prayer and personal revelation. Most importantly, it brought me to discover the sweetness and security encompassed in a growing relationship with our Father.

Although I now recognize that length of prayer is a personal matter, and therefore I will not suggest a specific length for others, in this case the teacher's challenge proved to be the impetus I needed to improve my prayers. Through the years as I have honored this commitment I believe I have begun to know God. I feel more confident about my ability to speak with him and to understand his revelations to me. Coming to this point has been worth every effort I have put forth. I cherish the hope that as I continue to pursue this goal of having daily communication with my Father, one day I will come to know him and to be like him. (See 1 John 3:1-2.) Knowing God requires that we come to recognize his voice, receive his Spirit, and realize his presence.

PROGRESSIVE REWARDS FROM PRAYER

It is through prayer that we learn to approach and converse with God, acquire the ability to listen to him, and develop the skill of understanding and working with his Spirit. Prayer is like a ladder. As we make the effort to climb each step, the Lord opens to our view new horizons of progress and knowledge.

Consider Christ's appearance in ancient America. As the people partook of the presence of their Savior, they experienced a spiritual yearning to be baptized, to receive the Holy Ghost, and to keep the commandments. The Savior, knowing the sincerity of their commitment, gave them what may be his greatest sermon, so far as our records go. Note that, as recorded in 3 Nephi 19, when he came the next day he used prayer as a means to prepare the people and as an instrument for instruction.

> They [the twelve chosen disciples] knelt again and prayed to the Father in the name of Jesus. And they did pray for that which they

most desired; and they desired that the Holy Ghost should be given unto them. (3 Nephi 19:8-9.)

After this prayer the twelve were baptized, and then they received the baptism of the Spirit in a rich outpouring. Their prayer had been answered in a magnificent way. This Holy Spirit is the instrument through which Church members receive and understand all communication from God, and its presence is intensified by daily effective prayer.

The record says Jesus again commanded the disciples to pray.

And behold, they began to pray; . . . And it came to pass that Jesus . . . bowed himself to the earth and he said: Father, I thank thee that thou hast given the Holy Ghost unto these whom I have chosen; . . . Father, I pray thee that thou wilt give the Holy Ghost unto all them that shall believe in their words. Father, thou hast given them the Holy Ghost because they believe in me; and thou seest that they believe in me because *thou hearest them.* (3 Nephi 19:19-22; italics added.)

Notice the Savior's repeated emphasis on the importance of having the Holy Ghost. Notice also that his simple statement "Thou hearest them" evidences his confidence that God listens to sincere prayers.

. . . And it came to pass that when Jesus had thus prayed unto the Father, he came unto his disciples, and behold, they did still continue, without ceasing, to pray unto him; and they did not multiply many words, for *it was given unto them what they should pray,* and they were filled with desire. (3 Nephi 19:24; italics added.)

Here we observe the principle that "it was given unto them what they should pray." This suggests the disciples had developed the ability to unite their desires with the Lord's will. This prepared them for the next event.

And it came to pass that Jesus blessed them as they did pray unto him; and his countenance did smile upon them, and the light of his countenance did shine upon them, and behold they were as white as the countenance and also the garments of Jesus; and behold the whiteness thereof did exceed all the whiteness, yea, even there could be nothing upon earth so white as the whiteness thereof.

And Jesus said unto them: Pray on; nevertheless they did not cease to pray.

And he turned from them again, and went a little way off and bowed himself to the earth; and he prayed again unto the Father, saying:

Father, I thank thee that thou hast purified those whom I have chosen, because of their faith. . . .

And when Jesus had spoken these words he came again unto his disciples; and behold they did pray steadfastly, without ceasing, unto him; and he did smile upon them again; and behold they were white, even as Jesus.

And it came to pass that he went again a little way off and prayed unto the Father;

And tongue cannot speak the words which he prayed, neither can be written by man the words which he prayed.

And the multitude did hear and do bear record; and their hearts were open and they did understand in their hearts the words which he prayed.

Nevertheless, so great and marvelous were the words which he prayed that they cannot be written, neither can they be uttered by man." (3 Nephi 19:25-28, 30-34.)

By examining these passages, we witness the role prayer played in preparing the people for further truth. Prayer prefaced the disciples' baptism and their receipt of the Holy Ghost. As the disciples followed Christ's commandment to pray, they were purified. Ultimately through prayer the hearts of the multitude were opened to the extent that they understood the "great and marvelous" words Christ spoke to his Father. God desires likewise to share inspiring messages with us, and will do so to the extent that we can receive them. These are available to all who have the Spirit, who love the Lord, and who seek to purify themselves. (See D&C 76:114-119.) As we acquire these traits, the Lord will reveal to our minds great knowledge and understanding. These revelations will come line upon line, and we will grow into the principle of revelation and thereby come to know God better.

LEVELS OF PRAYER

To aid us in perfecting our prayer skills, let's analyze three basic levels of prayer. Notice the characteristics of each and the differences between one level and the next. Try to determine which level your prayers are on and what you need to learn, change, and work on to perfect them.

Level one can be described as mechanical or ritualistic prayer. The motions are evident and the words are said, but the heart and mind are dwelling on something else. This kind of prayer is usually said when one is tired, rushed, or preoccupied. We tend to go through the motions of prayer because we can't face ourselves with a clear conscience if we haven't "prayed." But if our goal is to communicate with God, mechanical prayer will never do.

Level two depicts a prayer in which the heart and mind are present but the thoughts and intents belong to the individual not to the Lord. Typically on this level no preparation takes place before prayer—the person does all the talking, he does not meaningfully seek the Lord's will, and he does not listen for answers during or after his prayer. This person's prayers usually reach their peak of intensity when he faces a crisis.

Level three portrays a prayer wherein preparation precedes the prayer—the person sincerely expresses gratitude; he ponders; he seeks the Spirit's promptings; he awaits the Lord's will; and he makes commitments. His relationship with God is strengthened by his coming to know God better.

As I conclude this book, I ask each of you, the readers, to strive to draw nearer to God by improving your skills in prayer and in receiving personal revelation. To help you meet this request, I suggest a method which helped me—that of spending a specified length of time in communicating with the Lord every day for two weeks. In the light of our discussion, choose that length of time yourself. I testify that by devoting quality time in this way you will experience the joy of strengthening your relationship with your Father. You will come to know him better.

GOALS AND STEPS

A few other suggestions may assist you in accomplishing this long-term goal:

1. Decide where you are in relation to where you want to be in your prayer life. Then set goals and prepare a plan to achieve them.

2. Check chapter titles and make a list of the steps we have discussed. Refer to them before prayer. Adapt the steps to your own style. Don't become too rigid. Allow the Spirit to intervene and influence your feelings and expressions.

3. Schedule the same time of day for prayer each day. Decide on a time when your faculties are alert and responsive. It is impossible to experience communication when you are tired. I suggest a time in the morning when you are fresh, before the day has left you weary or upset. Perhaps you may want to arise earlier for this purpose.

Here are a few specific suggestions if you decide to try my recommendation for the two-week longer-prayer experiment:

1. Dedicate the entire time. For the first few days you may run out of things to say. If this happens, stay on your knees and ponder for the remainder of the time. Pondering is an important part of prayer. It allows the Lord an opportunity to speak. Don't feel you need to be talking all the time in order to offer an effective prayer.

2. Spend more time if you desire. Don't feel that after one longer session in the morning you don't need to approach the Lord again until bedtime. Pray when an urge comes to talk to the Lord. Usually you have yearnings to pray because you have an abundance of the Spirit with you. Taking advantage of these

situations will make it easier to communicate with the Lord and to understand his revelations to you.

THE CHALLENGE

Our challenge is before us. Our happiness in this life and for eternity depends on our coming to know God. On these terms, our Heavenly Father offers us everything he has. He lovingly pleads:

> Draw near unto me and I will draw near unto you; seek me diligently and ye shall find me; ask and ye shall receive; knock, and it shall be opened unto you. (D&C 88:63.)

Dedicating time each day to develop our relationship with our Father will affect our actions each day and, ultimately, how we spend eternity. It is a small price to pay for the eternal happiness he offers us.

Index

foundation for, 7-12
gratitude expressed, 17-22, 23-28
happiness through, 3
increased in time of need, 20-21
levels of, 88-89
listening during, 40-49
Marion G. Romney on, 3-4
no response to, 38-39
perfection through, 4
preparation for, 7-12, 42-43
progressive rewards from, 85-87
remaining on knees after, 76-79
requests, 35-39
role of exaltation, 3
secret, 8
skill in, 4
Spencer W. Kimball on, 8, 13
Truman G. Madsen on, 27
Preparation, for prayer, 7-12, 42-43
Priesthood, revelation on, 33-34
Privacy, 8
Promptings, 32-33

— R —

Repentance, importance to prayer, 15-16
Revelation, Bruce R. McConkie on, 33
importance of following, 64-65
in minds and hearts, 54
on priesthood, 33-34
Rigdon, Sidney, 9, 77
Romney, Marion G., on prayer, 3-4

— S —

Scripture study, 10, 15, 70-71
Arthur Bassett on, 10
Marion D. Hanks on, 10
Scriptures, new editions, 70-71

Self-reliance, 46, 47
Simpson, Robert L., on commitment, 77
Sin, 15
discernment calloused by, 42
Smith, Hyrum, revelation to, 55
Smith, Joseph, 10
loss of manuscript, 38
on personal revelation, 58-59, 63
prayer of, 8
revelation to, 9, 55, 77
Smith, Joseph F., revelation to, 9
Stewardship, 66-69
Still small voice, 55
Stupor of thought, 56

— T —

Testimony, 50
Testimony meeting, 24
Thankfulness, 17-28
See also Gratitude
Thanksgivings, to the Lord, 25
Trials, 68-69
increased prayer during, 20-21
Trust, of the Lord, 39

— U —

United Order, 68

— V —

Visiting teaching, 31-32

— Y —

Young, Brigham, on following prophet,
64-65
on God, 82